LIVING GOD'S WORD

YEAR B

DAVID KNIGHT

LIVING GOD'S WORD

Reflections on the Weekly Gospels

YEAR B

ST. ANTHONY MESSENGER PRESS

Cincinnati, Ohio

Cover design and illustrations by Karla Ann Sheppard
Book design by Mary Alfieri

ISBN 0-86716-307-0

Published by St. Anthony Messenger Press
Printed in the U.S.A.

Contents

Lent

Easter Triduum and Easter

Ordinary Time (Tenth Sunday of the Year Through Thirty-Fourth Sunday of the Year)

Solemnities of the Lord During the Season of the Year

Other Solemnities and Feasts Which Replace Sunday

Feasts and Saints' Days

LITURGICAL CALENDAR

Liturgical Calendar

	1999 (A)	2000 (B)	2001(C)
1st Sunday of Advent	11/29/98	11/28/99	12/3/00
2nd Sunday of Advent	12/6/98	12/5/99	12/10/00
3rd Sunday of Advent	12/13/98	12/12/99	12/17/00
4th Sunday of Advent	12/20/98	12/19/99	12/24/00
Christmas	12/25/98	12/25/99	12/25/00
Holy Family	12/27/98	12/26/99	12/31/00
Octave of Christmas	1/1/99	1/1/00	1/1/01
Epiphany	1/3/99	1/2/00	1/7/01
Baptism of the Lord	1/10/99	1/9/00	1/8/01**
2nd Sunday of the Year	1/17/99	1/16/00	1/14/01
3rd Sunday of the Year	1/24/99	1/23/00	1/21/01
4th Sunday of the Year	1/31/99	1/30/00	1/28/01
5th Sunday of the Year	2/7/99	2/6/00	2/4/01
6th Sunday of the Year	2/14/99	2/13/00	2/11/01
7th Sunday of the Year	——	2/20/00	2/18/01
8th Sunday of the Year	——	2/27/00*	2/25/01
Ash Wednesday	2/17/99	3/8/00	2/28/01
First Sunday of Lent	2/21/99	3/12/00	3/4/01
Second Sunday of Lent	2/28/99	3/19/00	3/11/01
Third Sunday of Lent	3/7/99	3/26/00	3/18/01
Fourth Sunday of Lent	3/14/99	4/2/00	3/25/01
Fifth Sunday of Lent	3/21/99	4/9/00	4/1/01
Palm/Passion Sunday	3/28/99	4/16/00	4/8/01
Easter	4/4/99	4/23/00	4/15/01
Second Sunday of Easter	4/11/99	4/30/00	4/22/01
Third Sunday of Easter	4/18/99	5/7/00	4/29/01
Fourth Sunday of Easter	4/25/99	5/14/00	5/6/01
Fifth Sunday of Easter	5/2/99	5/21/00	5/13/01
Sixth Sunday of Easter	5/9/99	5/28/00	5/20/01
Ascension (Thursday)	5/13/99	6/1/00	5/24/01
Seventh Sunday of Easter	5/16/99	6/4/00	5/27/01
Pentecost	5/23/99	6/11/00	6/3/01

2002 (A)	2003 (B)	2004 (C)	2005 (A)	2006 (B)	2007 (C)
12/2/01	12/1/02	11/30/03	11/28/04	11/27/05	12/3/06
12/9/01	12/8/02	12/7/03	12/5/04	12/4/05	12/10/06
12/16/01	12/15/02	12/14/03	12/12/04	12/11/05	12/17/06
12/23/01	12/22/02	12/21/03	12/19/04	12/18/05	12/24/06
12/25/01	12/25/02	12/25/03	12/25/04	12/25/05	12/25/06
12/30/01	12/29/02	12/28/03	12/26/04	12/30/05	12/31/06
1/1/02	1/1/03	1/1/04	1/1/05	1/1/06	1/1/07
1/6/02	1/5/03	1/4/04	1/2/05	1/8/06	1/7/07
1/13/02	1/12/03	1/11/04	1/9/05	1/9/06**	1/8/07**
1/20/02	1/19/03	1/18/04	1/16/05	1/15/06	1/14/07
1/27/02	1/26/03	1/25/04	1/23/05	1/22/06	1/21/07
2/3/02	2/2/03	2/1/04	1/30/05	1/29/06	1/28/07
2/10/02	2/9/03	2/8/04	2/6/05	2/5/06	2/4/07
——	2/16/03	2/15/04	——	2/12/06	2/11/07
——	2/23/03	2/22/04	——	2/19/06	2/18/07
——	3/2/03	——	——	2/26/06	——
2/13/02	3/5/03	2/25/04	2/9/05	3/1/06	2/21/07
2/17/02	3/9/03	2/29/04	2/13/05	3/5/06	2/25/07
2/24/02	3/16/03	3/7/04	2/20/05	3/12/06	3/4/07
3/3/02	3/23/03	3/14/04	2/27/05	3/19/06	3/11/07
3/10/02	3/30/03	3/21/04	3/6/05	3/26/06	3/18/07
3/17/02	4/6/03	3/28/04	3/13/05	4/2/06	3/25/07
3/24/02	4/13/03	4/4/04	3/20/05	4/9/06	4/1/07
3/31/02	4/20/03	4/11/04	3/27/05	4/16/06	4/8/07
4/7/02	4/27/03	4/18/04	4/3/05	4/23/06	4/15/07
4/14/02	5/4/03	4/25/04	4/10/05	4/30/06	4/22/07
4/21/02	5/11/03	5/2/04	4/17/05	5/7/06	4/29/07
4/28/02	5/18/03	5/9/04	4/24/05	5/14/06	5/6/07
5/5/02	5/25/03	5/16/04	5/1/05	5/21/06	5/13/07
5/9/02	5/29/03	5/20/04	5/5/05	5/25/06	5/17/07
5/12/02	6/1/03	5/23/04	5/8/05	5/28/06	5/20/07
5/19/02	6/8/03	5/30/04	5/15/05	6/4/06	5/27/07

Feast of the Holy Family falls on Friday, December 30, 2005.
** Baptism of the Lord moves to Monday in these years.
* 9th Week of the Year precedes Ash Wednesday in 2000.

Liturgical Calendar

	1999 (A)	2000 (B)	2001(C)
Week of the Year	8th	10th	9th
Trinity Sunday	5/30/99	6/18/00	6/10/01
Week of the Year	9th	11th	10th
Body and Blood of Christ	6/6/99	6/25/00	6/17/01
Week of the Year	10th	12th	11th
Sacred Heart (Friday)	6/11/99	6/30/00	6/22/01
9th Sunday of the Year	——	3/5/00	——
10th Sunday of the Year	——	——	——
11th Sunday of the Year	6/13/99	——	——
12th Sunday of the Year	6/20/99	——	6/24/01
13th Sunday of the Year	6/27/99	7/2/00	7/1/01
14th Sunday of the Year	7/4/99	7/9/00	7/8/01
15th Sunday of the Year	7/11/99	7/16/00	7/15/01
16th Sunday of the Year	7/18/99	7/23/00	7/22/01
17th Sunday of the Year	7/25/99	7/30/00	7/29/01
18th Sunday of the Year	8/1/99	8/6/00	8/5/01
19th Sunday of the Year	8/8/99	8/13/00	8/12/01
20th Sunday of the Year	8/15/99	8/20/00	8/19/01
21st Sunday of the Year	8/22/99	8/27/00	8/26/01
22nd Sunday of the Year	8/29/99	9/3/00	9/2/01
23rd Sunday of the Year	9/5/99	9/10/00	9/9/01
24th Sunday of the Year	9/12/99	9/17/00	9/16/01
25th Sunday of the Year	9/19/99	9/24/00	9/23/01
26th Sunday of the Year	9/26/99	10/1/00	9/30/01
27th Sunday of the Year	10/3/99	10/8/00	10/7/01
28th Sunday of the Year	10/10/99	10/15/00	10/14/01
29th Sunday of the Year	10/17/99	10/22/00	10/21/01
30th Sunday of the Year	10/24/99	10/29/00	10/28/01
31st Sunday of the Year	10/31/99	11/5/00	11/4/01
32nd Sunday of the Year	11/7/99	11/12/00	11/11/01
33rd Sunday of the Year	11/14/99	11/19/00	11/18/01
Christ the King	11/21/99	11/26/00	11/25/01

2002 (A)	2003 (B)	2004 (C)	2005 (A)	2006 (B)	2007 (C)
7th	10th	9th	7th	9th	8th
5/26/02	6/15/03	6/6/04	5/22/05	6/11/06	6/3/07
8th	11th	10th	8th	10th	9th
6/2/02	6/22/03	6/13/04	5/29/05	6/18/06	6/10/07
9th	12th	11th	9th	11th	10th
6/7/02	6/27/03	6/18/04	6/3/05	6/23/06	6/15/07
6/9/02	—	—	6/5/05	—	—
6/16/02	—	—	6/12/05	—	6/17/07
6/23/02	—	6/20/04	6/19/05	6/25/06	6/24/07
6/30/02	6/29/03	6/27/04	6/26/05	7/2/06	7/1/07
7/7/02	7/6/03	7/4/04	7/3/05	7/9/06	7/8/07
7/14/02	7/13/03	7/11/04	7/10/05	7/16/06	7/15/07
7/21/02	7/20/03	7/18/04	7/17/05	7/23/06	7/22/07
7/28/02	7/27/03	7/25/04	7/24/05	7/30/06	7/29/07
8/4/02	8/3/03	8/1/04	7/31/05	8/6/06	8/5/07
8/11/02	8/10/03	8/8/04	8/7/05	8/13/06	8/12/07
8/18/02	8/17/03	8/15/04	8/14/05	8/20/06	8/19/07
8/25/02	8/24/03	8/22/04	8/21/05	8/27/06	8/26/07
9/1/02	8/31/03	8/29/04	8/28/05	9/3/06	9/2/07
9/8/02	9/7/03	9/5/04	9/4/05	9/10/06	9/9/07
9/15/02	9/14/03	9/12/04	9/11/05	9/17/06	9/16/07
9/22/02	9/21/03	9/19/04	9/18/05	9/24/06	9/23/07
9/29/02	9/28/03	9/26/04	9/25/05	10/1/06	9/30/07
10/6/02	10/5/03	10/3/04	10/2/05	10/8/06	10/7/07
10/13/02	10/12/03	10/10/04	10/9/05	10/15/06	10/14/07
10/20/02	10/19/03	10/17/04	10/16/05	10/22/06	10/21/07
10/27/02	10/26/03	10/24/04	10/23/05	10/29/06	10/28/07
11/3/02	11/2/03	10/31/04	10/30/05	11/5/06	11/4/07
11/10/02	11/9/03	11/7/04	11/6/05	11/12/06	11/11/07
11/17/02	11/16/03	11/14/04	11/13/05	11/19/06	11/18/07
11/24/02	11/23/03	11/21/04	11/20/05	11/26/06	11/25/07

Introduction

> *"By means of sacred scripture, read during the
> liturgy of the word and explained during the homily,
> 'God speaks to his people, revealing the mystery of
> their redemption and salvation and offering them
> spiritual nourishment. Through his word, Christ
> himself is present in the assembly of his people.'
> Thus the Church at Mass 'receives the bread of life
> from the table of God's word and unceasingly offers
> it to the faithful.'"*[1]

There is mystery to ponder in these lines from the
Introduction to the *Lectionary for Mass*. But, in
practice, listening to the readings at Sunday Mass can
be frustrating. We frequently do not understand them. And
the more we do understand, the more we would like time to
reflect on them and absorb them—time not provided during
Mass. We are left feeling incomplete.

This is not only frustrating; it is dangerous. If our only
exposure to Scripture is at Sunday Mass and if we do not
understand what we hear, we will conclude, as many
Catholics have, that we "just don't understand" the Bible.
The obvious answer to this—"How can you understand it if
you don't read it?"—is countered by, "I hear it on Sundays,
and I don't understand it." So the danger is that we will not
ever begin reading the Bible because our experience of it at
Sunday Mass has been uninspiring or even frustrating.

This book will not change all of that, but it can help.

Typically, the liturgy includes four biblical passages
on Sunday. A Gospel passage is the centerpiece; preceding
it are a reading from the Old Testament, a psalm prayed or
sung as a response and a passage from another of the New
Testament writings.

This book will tell you what the readings are so that each

week, if you desire, you can look them over ahead of time, see the context in which they are found, call someone you know to ask about anything you don't understand, and come to Mass on Sunday prepared to sit back, enjoy and absorb what you hear.

I have been publishing weekly reflections like these in my Sunday bulletin for ten years. I began writing them because I remembered telling someone the year I graduated from high school that I could not remember one homily that had been preached in my parish church my whole life long. (In those days they were called sermons.) My experience was that, even if what was said in church inspired me momentarily, I never thought about it again once Mass was over. As a result, any seed planted in my mind died before it had a chance to root itself in my heart through decisions. The fault was not in the preacher; it was in the fact that I never took time to think about what I had heard.

I began publishing in the parish bulletin the main thoughts of my homilies in the hope that someone might read and reflect on them. And the feedback from the people was very good. Several told me they were sticking the bulletin on their refrigerator door and using it for meditation all during the week, especially the reflections on the daily readings.

All the reflections in these pages are based on the Gospel of the particular Sunday or weekday. I frequently approach the Gospel asking what light it casts on a particular question. For example, I might ask for several weeks in a row what the Gospel for the Sunday tells us about Baptism or another sacrament. When I do this, my concern is to find what there is in the reading itself, in its true meaning and interpretation, that relates to the topic at hand. The reflections are homilies; that is, reflections on the Scripture readings themselves, not sermons that develop topics for their own sake. But I have found that to approach any passage of Scripture with a question drawn from one's present concerns or experience of life is a way to discover in the text rich veins of meaning previously unmined.

How to Use This Book

I suggest that you read the reflection on the Sunday Gospel first. Ask yourself what this Gospel or this reflection says to you, what meaning it has for you. Then ask yourself what you intend to do about it.

In the section entitled "Living This Week's Gospels," I offer for each week five suggested responses you can make to the Gospel. These are based on five words which summarize our identity as Christians. Every one of us is a Christian by belief in Jesus Christ as Savior. And every one of us is called to be a disciple, which means to lead a life characterized by reflection on the teaching and example of Jesus, the Master of the Way.

In addition, at Baptism each of us was anointed with chrism and consecrated by God to continue Jesus' work as Prophet, Priest and King. These three words give us our job description as Christians.

Each week therefore offers a suggestion about how to express and live out our belief in Jesus as Savior and as Teacher (being a Christian and a disciple); how to bear witness to him in action (being a prophet); how to minister to others and nurture them (sharing in his priesthood); and how to work for the extension of his reign over every area and activity of human life (being responsible stewards of his kingship). No one could possibly live out all of these suggestions all the time, but you might try each one for a day. Or pick one and work at it all week.

For each day of the week I have chosen one line from the day's Gospel and offered one question to stimulate reflection. The ideal, of course, would be to read the whole Gospel passage for yourself—or, if your schedule permits, go to daily Mass and get it live! But in today's busy world, you may have only time to read one line and to think about one question whenever you can during the day.

Finally, there is a prayer that you can say each day all week, asking for the grace to live by the values proposed in the Sunday reflection. Repeated prayer increases desire.

Drawing People Together

Christian discipleship is both personal and communal. We grow in grace together. We nourish our hearts while we nourish the hearts of others. And so you could use this book to draw closer to others in the communion of the Holy Spirit while you yourself draw closer to God.

Invite someone to read the reflections with you and talk about them. Ask such questions as, "What does this say to you? How do you feel about it? What do you think you could do in response to it?" If you do this with family or close friends, it will raise the level of your interaction and deepen your understanding of each other. If you invite acquaintances, you will turn them into friends.

The Sunday Readings

The Sunday readings are presented in a three-year cycle (Years A, B and C). Over the course of the three years we hear the main sections of all four Gospels: Matthew in Year A, Mark in Year B (this volume), Luke in Year C. We hear the Gospel according to John during the Easter season of all three years and on a few other Sundays during the Christmas and Lenten seasons. In Year B, instead of Mark's version of the multiplication of the loaves, the liturgy inserts John's, along with its following teaching about the Bread of Life.

The Old Testament readings for Sundays were chosen individually because they relate in some way to the theme of the Gospel. They are presented as isolated passages, not book by book. There is no sequence or pattern in the order in which the books from the Old Testament appear. What we should be alert to, therefore, is the unity between the Old and New Testament readings, which becomes visible to us when we see how events or themes in both of them are related to each other.

The selections from other New Testament writings (Acts, the Letters and the Book of Revelation) are read "semicontinuously," that is, the main passages from one letter or book are presented sequentially. Because the readings from each book are presented as a block, it is possible to study each one as a whole during the period when selections from it are being read at Mass.

The Sunday and weekday liturgies together expose us to 128 of the 150 Psalms. The verses we use as responsorial chants are chosen to be responses to the readings they follow.

The Weekday Readings

The weekday readings are not geared to match the Sunday readings at all; they are a completely independent selection. Instead of an ABC cycle, there is a two-year cycle for the weekday readings (Year I and Year II). Only the first reading changes; the weekday Gospels are the same every year. To help us easily remember what year we are in, an odd-numbered year (like 1997, 1999) will always be Year I; Year II will always be a number divisible by two (1998, 2000).

During the Season of the Year or Ordinary Time, the weekday Gospels begin with the first one to be written, Mark (Weeks 1-9), and go straight through selected passages from Matthew (Weeks 10-21) and Luke (Weeks 22-34). Daily participation in the Eucharist gives us a tour of these three Gospels (the Synoptics) every year.

About half the selections for the first reading on weekdays come from the Old Testament. There is no precise order in the way the books are presented—Old and New Testament readings are interspersed during the year with no obvious guiding pattern—but, with a few exceptions all the readings from each book will be given consecutively. We can therefore study each book in turn while selections from it are read at Mass. In a given year, the Old Testament books are presented approximately in the order in which they were written. All of the Old Testament books except Obadiah and Judith and all of the New Testament books are represented in the readings.

During special seasons (Advent, Christmas, Lent and Easter) the themes of the season determine the choice of readings.

Special feasts and saints' days also have their own

readings, which replace the weekday and sometimes the Sunday readings. Reflections for these special feasts are in a section of their own.

A liturgical calendar or church bulletin will aid tremendously in helping to match the date with the corresponding reflection. (See page x.)

"A Fountain of Renewal"

The introduction to the Roman *Lectionary for Mass* begins:

> The Church loves sacred scripture and is anxious to deepen its understanding of the truth and to nourish its own life by studying these sacred writings. The Second Vatican Council likened the bible to a fountain of renewal within the community of God's people and directed that in the revision of liturgical celebrations there should be "more abundant, varied and appropriate reading from sacred scripture." The council further directed that at Mass "the treasures of the bible should be opened up more lavishly so that richer fare might be provided for the faithful at the table of God's word. In this way a more representative portion of sacred scripture will be read to the people over a set cycle of years."[2]

That is the motive and prayer behind the writing of this book.

Notes

[1] Introduction, #1, *Lectionary for Mass*, copyright © 1970 by International Commission on English in the Liturgy. Used with permission.

[2] Ibid.

ADVENT SEASON

First Sunday of Advent

Giving Up Control: Blessed Are the Poor in Spirit

Isaiah 63:16-17, 19; 64:2-7; 1 Corinthians 1:3-9; Mark 13:33-37

This Gospel seems to say we should take control of ourselves: "Be on guard! Stay awake!" In reality it is a summons to abandon control—or to abandon the kind of control we spontaneously want to have over our lives.

What does it mean to be "awake" or "watchful" or "ready" for the Lord when he comes? It means to be ready to surrender to him, to hear his voice, to do his will, to "let it be done unto us according to his word" and to rejoice in that word, whatever it is. It means to be using all that we have and are in his service, and to be waiting in expectation for him as the bride waits for the bridegroom.

In the present moment, this means keeping our hearts in union with Jesus: our thoughts in harmony with his thoughts, our desires in harmony with his desires, our wills in harmony with everything he said and taught and did to be for us "the Way, the Truth and the Life." It means to be constantly attuning ourselves to him the way a musician attunes one instrument to another—that is, to listen to the note we have just played (the thought we have just had, the desire just felt, the words just said, the decision we have just made) and to "bounce it off" the Heart of Jesus, listening for the echo, to see if our hearts are in harmony with his.

The prerequisite for this is true and deep humility—which does not mean thinking badly of ourselves, or putting ourselves down. True humility means "being peaceful with the truth," including both the truth of our goodness and beauty, and the truth of our inadequacy. Where our inadequacy is concerned, it means being peaceful with the fact that we are simply and radically unable to make

ourselves happy alone, or even—left to ourselves alone—
to become as beautiful, as good, or as beneficial to others
in this world as we are called to be, as we desire to be. It
means being "poor in spirit," which is the condition of those
who know they haven't got it made. Those who know this
are open to something—to someone—more.

Being poor in spirit is a blessing, our Lord teaches,
because it makes us open to receive, to accept, the reign of
God. If I know that I myself do not have the answers I need,
the light I need, the love I need, the strength I need; if I
know that within myself I simply do not have the resources I
need to be happy, to be loving, to be generous and given to
others in this world, then I am open to Jesus who comes as
Savior, as Light of the world, as the Way, the Truth and the
Life. I am open to his reign over me. I am ready to surrender.
I am ready to give up control, and to give it up to him.

Anything that is a "power trip" closes us, for that
moment—or to that extent—to the influence of Christ in our
lives. When we are conscious of our own power or ability—
exulting in it, trusting in it, delivering ourselves over to the
unrestrained exercise of it—our attitude is not one of
openness to the reign of Christ over us, not a listening
attitude, eager to hear his voice and follow it. In the middle
of a power trip we do not listen to anything but the surging
energy within us. We do not follow anything but the pinging
of our own guidance system and the direction of our own
desires. We are like a charging bull or a bullet that has left
the gun. We are on our own. And we want to be.

Advent is a time to be aware of our inadequacy, of
the destructiveness of the directions we take when we are
"on our own." It is a time to renounce all "power trips"—
all confidence in economic power, in military power, in
the power of our social status and prestige. It is a time to
reexamine any power we have over others, and to surrender
it over to the Lord of our lives, asking and striving to use it
only in response, in obedience to his will. It is a time to
examine the use we make of our talents, our position, our
resources, and to give up control.

Reflecting on This Week's Gospels

First Week of Advent

Pray daily: Lord, you came as the teacher of life, the master of the way. Teach me the way of trust and dependence on you. Free me from enslavement to my own power.

Monday: Matthew 8:5-11. The centurion said in reply, "Lord, I am not worthy to have you come under my roof; but only speak the word, and my servant will be healed." What power did this pagan Roman officer, a man of the world, recognize in Jesus? Where do you see this power?

Tuesday: Luke 10:21-24. "[Y]ou have hidden these things from the wise and the intelligent and have revealed them to infants." Are you as willing to learn from God or about God as a little child is? Are you as open to changes?

Wednesday: Matthew 15:29-37. "Great crowds came to him, bringing with them the lame, the maimed, the blind, the mute, and many others." Which seem to be more attracted to religion: those who feel they have their lives under control, or those who do not? How would you describe yourself?

Thursday: Matthew 7:21, 24-27. "And everyone who hears these words of mine and does not act on them will be like a foolish man who built his house on sand." How often do you act consciously and explicitly on the words of Jesus? On what do you rely for security?

Friday: Matthew 9:27-31. "Two blind men approached Jesus. He said to them, "Do you believe that I am able to do this?" What do you believe Jesus can do for you? What are you asking him to do?

Saturday: Matthew 9:35 to 10:1, 6-8. "When he saw the crowds, he had compassion for them, because they were harassed and helpless, like sheep without a shepherd." Do these words make you think of the rich and powerful, or of the poor and powerless? Why?

Living This Week's Gospels

As Christian: Write down three areas of your life over which you feel you do not have sufficient control. Ask Jesus to act in these areas as your Savior.

As Disciple: Each day in Advent read a few lines of the Gospels, expecting them to cast light on your daily life. Ask how they do.

As Prophet: During Advent wear or put where you work some visible symbol which proclaims the expectation of your heart.

As Priest: Ask a couple of people you work with or associate with how they observe Advent, or what it means to them.

As King: Work against the custom of getting into the Christmas season during Advent. For example, try to put off Christmas decorations and parties until Christmas.

Second Sunday of Advent

Openness to Change:
Blessed Are Those Who Mourn

Isaiah 40:1-5, 9-11; 2 Peter 3:8-14; Mark 1:1-8

A ny new beginning means accepting change. Growth presupposes change. And any acceptance of Jesus Christ—or any deeper, more fulfilling acceptance of him—takes place in an act of simultaneously opening and delivering ourselves to change.

When John the Baptizer appeared on the scene "proclaiming a baptism of repentance," he was preaching change. He was saying that only change can "lead to the forgiveness of sins." And only change can lead us deeper into relationship with Jesus Christ; only change can free us from what holds us back from the fullness of life; only change can open us to the clarity his light gives to our lives, to the joy his love brings to individuals and families, to working days and weekends. Only change can make peace possible in the world. Change is the price we pay for life.

The strange thing is that we fear change more than pain! Psychologists say that animals will change their habits rather than endure pain, but humans won't. I heard this in a class and did not believe it. Years later I asked a practicing psychologist about it, who said, "I see that every day! People will endure the pain of an unsatisfying marriage for years rather than open themselves to changes by seeking counseling." Many people prefer to endure physical pain as long as they can instead of seeing a doctor and perhaps having to adapt to an unknown diagnosis or treatment. How many times have we all chosen to put up with some pain or dissatisfaction we are used to rather than take the risk of making a major change in our lives?

What is behind this is fear of the unknown; fear of

facing something we do not want to face; fear of knowing something we do not want to know; fear of a challenge we may not want to meet. We make a proverb of the ostrich who buries its head in the ground at the approach of danger in order to feel safe, but we do the same thing. We "put our heads under the pillow" by burying ourselves in distractions: in TV, in work, in talk with others, in anything that blocks out the questions we do not want to hear, the options we do not want to think about. We make sure we do not have time to pray.

That is why the spiritual life is always, in some sense and to some degree, a call to "go out into the desert." There are voices that cry in the desert—voices like that of John proclaiming the good news of change, the good news of repentance and "life to the full." Voices that cannot be heard in the "city," where there are bright lights to blind us and street bustle to deafen us and idols available to take the place of God.

When Jesus says, "Blessed are those who mourn, for they will be comforted," he is inviting us to go out into the desert, to listen to the voices we think we do not want to hear, to open ourselves to that wind of change which is the gentle breeze or the roaring tornado of the Holy Spirit. He is saying, "Look at those things you are afraid of, think the thoughts you are suppressing, face the pain, the dissatisfaction in your life: there is a solution!" Blessed are those who face all the things they have to mourn, for they—and they alone—will find peace, will find comfort, will find joy.

This is not just good psychological advice. The promise of Jesus is not based on the good, homey wisdom that it is better to face reality than to bury your head in the sand. The assurance of comfort Jesus gives is a promise he makes only because "the reign of God is at hand." Jesus does not say just because we face our problems everything will be all right. He says that redemption, deliverance, healing, the fullness of life is at hand; that all this is present in our world now, is offered—he offers it. There is comfort for those who face the truth of this world only if they believe in the truth of Christ.

And even then, only for those of us who are willing to open ourselves to change.

Reflecting on This Week's Gospels

Second Week of Advent

Pray daily: Lord, you came that we might have life and have it to the full. Teach me to look clearly at what diminishes my life, believing that through interaction with you all things can be turned into good.

Monday: Luke 5:17-26. Some men brought on a stretcher a man who was paralyzed. When Jesus saw their faith, he said, "Friend, your sins are forgiven you." Would you have preferred to hear these words or "Stand up and walk!"? Why? What afflicts you more: sickness, failure or distance from Christ?

Tuesday: Matthew 18:12-14. "If a shepherd has a hundred sheep and one of them has gone astray, does he not leave the ninety-nine on the mountains and go in search of the one that went astray?" What do you feel is most missing in your life? How are you going in search of it?

Wednesday: Matthew 11:28-30. "Take my yoke upon you and learn from me; for I am gentle and humble in heart, and you will find rest for your souls." What is the difference between taking Christ's yoke and learning from him? Which are you more conscious of doing?

Thursday: Matthew 11:11-15. "Let anyone with ears listen!" What is the difference between hearing Jesus' words and listening? Which do you do most often during Mass?

Friday: Matthew 11:16-19. "We played the flute for you, and you did not dance; / we wailed, and you did not mourn."

When have you reacted with feeling to something Jesus said? What seems to influence your reaction?

Saturday: Matthew 17:10-13. "Elijah has already come, and they did not recognize him, but they did to him whatever they pleased.... Then the disciples understood that he was speaking to them about John the Baptist." Are there things you have come to see in the Gospels that you did not understand before? Is this because you changed?

Living This Week's Gospels

As Christian: At the end of each day this week, look back and pick one thing that Jesus would want you to mourn over, one thing he would want you to rejoice in.

As Disciple: Try to think of some words or examples of Jesus that cast light on what you mourn over, what you rejoice in.

As Prophet: Visibly express in some way your mourning or your rejoicing each day. Try to express the Christian reason for it.

As Priest: Comfort someone who is mourning.

As King: Try to change one source of annoyance, anger, discouragement or sadness in the environment where you live or work.

Third Sunday of Advent

A New Way of Salvation: Blessed Are the Meek

Isaiah 61:1-2, 10-11; 1 Thessalonians 5:16-24;
John 1:6-8, 19-28

John the Baptizer was not the threat—or the scandal—
to people that Jesus was. He was finally killed by Herod
for saying things Herod did not want to hear, but the
people never turned against him as they turned against Jesus,
shouting, "Crucify him!"

The reason is that John fit the pattern of what he was.
He was a classic Old Testament prophet: an ascetic from the
desert who denounced evil fearlessly. People knew how to
relate to John. He met their expectations.

Jesus did not. As a Messiah, Jesus was a disappointment.
More than that: He was a disillusionment! When Pilate
brought him out, bound, beaten and delivered over to his
enemies, and said to the people, "Here is your king!", they
shouted, "Take him away! Crucify him!" They had finally
realized that Jesus was not going to use divine power to save
them from their oppressors, or to establish peace, justice and
prosperity on earth. That is when all their hope in him turned
to disappointment, and their disappointment turned into rage,
and they rejected him. And in them we rejected him too!

Another reason why John was acceptable is that John
radiated power, and people are attracted to power. John's
power was not political or physical, it was all personal and
spiritual, but it was power: the power of faith and of will
that made him such a fearsome ascetic. In contrast to John's,
the life-style of Jesus seemed bland! (See Matthew 9:14
and 11:18-19).

Jesus taught with the power of certain knowledge

(see Matthew 7:28-29), and he had power to heal and cast out demons. But this was not the power people expected—demanded—of the Messiah. They wanted a king who could and would use force to save them from their enemies. This is what Jesus refused to do. That is why they crucified him.

Jesus was rejected as Savior—and still is, although we are unwilling to recognize and acknowledge it—precisely because he would not use force, either human or divine, to impose the reign of God on earth as we would have him do: by stamping out crime and injustice. In our eyes, Jesus is a Savior who refuses to save us from anything, so what good is he?

We could, of course, accept Jesus as a purely spiritual Savior and say that redemption simply has nothing to do with civic life, economics, politics, or anything temporal or of this world; that the teachings of Jesus Christ can enlighten individuals in their private morality, but that he has nothing to say to nations or armies or multinational corporations.

If we do accept Jesus, however, as the one God sent to establish a kingdom, not *of* this world (see John 18:36) but *in* this world, "a kingdom of justice, love and peace" (Preface for the Feast of Christ the King), then we have to apply his teachings to public life as well as to private, and say that he is truly our Savior, not only in religious matters (narrowly understood), but also in economic and political affairs. To accept this, we would have to accept a whole new concept of "salvation"—precisely that concept which Jesus' own people (and we) refused to accept when the crowd began to shout, "Take him away! Crucify him!" This is the revolutionary concept of salvation without force, salvation through gentleness.

Jesus taught in the Beatitudes that the meek shall inherit the earth (see Matthew 5:5). Strange statement! We know from history and contemporary observation that the meek are usually the first to be dispossessed! It is not the gentle who succeed in defending their territory against aggressors; it is those with weapons who are willing to use them—like us!

But if we accept Jesus as the Savior he actually is, we have to accept his teachings as the way to save all of human life, including business and politics. Can you do this?

Reflecting on This Week's Gospels

Third Week of Advent

Pray daily: Lord, I believe in you as the Way, the Truth and the Life. Your way is the only way that saves. Your truth is valid against all the assumptions of our culture, our world. You alone give life to the full. Help me to follow you without reserve.

Monday: Matthew 21:23-27. They discussed this among themselves and said, "If we say, 'From heaven,' he will say to us, 'Why then did you not believe him?'" Do you believe that Jesus' teaching was truly from God? Could anyone ask you, "Then why don't you believe what he taught about gentleness?"

Tuesday: Matthew 21:28-32. Jesus said to them, "Truly I tell you, the tax collectors and the prostitutes are going into the kingdom of God ahead of you." Can you think of any group or category of people who seem to take the gospel more seriously than you do? Why is this?

Wednesday: Luke 7:18-23. John's disciples came to ask Jesus, "Are you the one who is to come, or are we to wait for another?" Are you waiting for some extraordinary intervention of God to change our world? Or do you believe that we can change it—and you can begin now—by using Jesus' method of powerless love?

Thursday: Luke 7:24-30. "What did you go out into the wilderness to look at? A reed shaken by the wind? ...Someone dressed in soft robes? ...A prophet?" What are you looking for in Jesus? In the Church? What do you really want?

Friday: John 5:33-36. "But I have a testimony greater than John's. The works that the Father has given me to complete, the very works that I am doing, testify on my behalf that the Father has sent me." What works of Jesus most effectively win you? What in other people most motivates you to change?

Saturday. *See readings for December 17-24.*

Living This Week's Gospels

As Christian: Make a list of the forces or actions you most depend on for security or success. Law enforcement? Security systems? Insurance? Physical fitness? People's opinions of you? Each day this week look at your attitude toward one of them, comparing it with your attitude toward Christ.

As Disciple: Each day this week take the attitude you are considering and try to remember or find something Jesus said (or did) in the Gospels which applies to it.

As Prophet: This week, each time you are treated unjustly or imposed upon, try responding with gentleness (of love, not passive aggression!) instead of with anger or a resort to power.

As Priest: This week, match every sign of respect you give to someone in power or authority with an explicit act that shows reverence for someone people consider less important than you.

As King: Notice how many signs, arrangements or policies where you live or shop or work express a reliance on power or intimidation. Suggest some concrete way to inject a note of gentleness into what is expressed.

Fourth Sunday of Advent

An Invitation to Desire: Blessed Are Those Who Hunger for Holiness

2 Samuel 7:1-5, 8b-11, 16; Romans 16:25-27; Luke 1:26-38

Why was the angel sent from God to the virgin whose name was Mary? Why precisely to this girl among all the young women of Israel? What "Sister said" to many of us in grade school (and what "Sister said" was the closest thing to working infallibility in the Catholic Church then, before or since!) was that God took flesh in Mary in answer to her desires.

Every girl in Israel, Sister said, dreamed of being the mother of the Messiah. But Mary wanted it most—most deeply, most passionately, with all her heart. So God chose her (having chosen her from the beginning, knowing how she would respond) and fulfilled her aching desire.

And so he set the pattern for us all: What brings God to earth, what brings him to birth in a heart, is desire. Blessed are those who desire, for they shall be fulfilled.

Not every desire is fulfilled, because not every desire is for fulfillment. Not every desire is for that which can fill us "to the full." That is why God does not satisfy every desire or answer every prayer. God sent Jesus that we might "have life and have it to the full" (John 10:10). If we do not want life to the full, our desires lack power with God. God loves too passionately to be seduced by moderate desire.

Mary the virgin is the model of human desire. Her whole being opened itself to love without limits; her whole soul to surrender without reserve. That is why her being above all others proclaimed the greatness of the Lord and her soul exulted in his fulfillment of her. In the measure that she desired it was given to her: full measure, pressed down, overflowing, overwhelming, everlasting. She confronted love with longing, power with vulnerability, fullness with emptiness, possessiveness with surrender, domination with abandonment, divinity with her humanity. If there was a contest, she won.

Because her desire was for more than this world can give, it was fulfilled by more than this world can accomplish: "The Holy Spirit will come upon you, and the power of the Most High will overshadow you; therefore the child to be born will be holy; he will be called Son of God." "Blessed are you among women. Blessed the fruit of your womb!"

This is the formula that brings salvation to the whole world—in all of its parts, in all of its nations, cultures, projects, undertakings and activities. The formula that saves the world is passionate desire for that which fulfills all desire. The formula that destroys the world—in all of its parts, in all of its nations, cultures, projects, undertakings and activities—is desire that settles for less.

Behind every sin, behind every destructive thought, word or action, is infinite desire despairing of fulfillment. Desire that is focused on pleasure is desire despairing of joy. Desire that is focused on money is desire despairing of happiness. Desire that is focused on power or prestige is desire despairing of love. All desires that are focused on this world or on anything in it are desires despairing of God. Any desire that narrows itself down to anything less than God is nothing but a masked despair of fulfillment. There is only one desire that has no trace of despair: "I know I am the servant of the Lord: let all be done to me according to his word!"

Fear is the mirror image of desire. What does the world, what do you, fear most at this moment? Is it loss of health or employment? Of relationship, of friends? Or the loss of fidelity to God? Is it the loss of something you desire? Or the loss of Desire itself? "Blessed are those who hunger and thirst for righteousness, for they will be filled."

Reflecting on This Week's Gospels

Fourth Week of Advent

Pray daily: Lord, my God, my being proclaims your infinite desire. My existence comes from your infinite desire to give yourself to me without limits. Let me feel the echo of this desire in my heart and love you without restraint.

December 17: Matthew 1:1-17. "So all the generations from Abraham to David are fourteen generations; and from David to the deportation to Babylon, fourteen generations; and from the deportation to Babylon to the Messiah, fourteen generations." Behind the world's history of initiatives, triumphs and defeats is the desire for fulfillment. Wisdom is the gift of appreciating what gives true fulfillment on earth. Do you long to learn from Jesus as the wisdom of God made flesh?

December 18: Matthew 1:18-24. "Joseph, son of David, do not be afraid to take Mary as your wife." Is your longing for a God who will intervene in your life, who will lead you and use you for his work, enough to overcome the awe and fear you feel at becoming involved with him?

December 19: Luke 1:5-25. The angel Gabriel said to Zechariah, "I have been sent to speak to you and to bring you this good news. But now, because you did not believe my words, which will be fulfilled in their time, you will become mute, unable to speak, until the day these things occur." Do you long to nurture the seed of God's word through reflection and prayer so that you might grow to knowledge and understanding and be able to speak his truth?

December 20: Luke 1:26-38. "[Y]ou will conceive in your womb and bear a son, and you will name him Jesus. He will be great and will be called the Son of the Most High, and the Lord God will give to him the throne of his ancestor David." Do you long for a human race delivered from all that divides it into hostile fragments? How much do you desire all races and cultures to be united as a single family in Christ?

December 21: Luke 1:39-45. "For as soon as I heard the sound of your greeting, the child in my womb leaped for joy." Do you believe God's light and life dawned anew in you at your Baptism? Do you long to bring to others the saving presence of his truth, his love in you?

December 22: Luke 1:46-56. "He has shown strength with his arm; / he has scattered the proud in the thoughts of their hearts. / He has brought down the powerful from their thrones, / and lifted up the lowly...." Do you believe that Jesus is overcoming the powerful of this world who put their personal good and the good of their particular countries over the good of the whole human race? Do you want to help him do this?

December 23: Luke 1:57-66. "On the eighth day they came to circumcise the child, and they were going to name him Zechariah after his father. But his mother said, 'No; he is to be called John.'" That name means "God is gracious," that is, a giver whose benevolent goodness shines out as beauty and attracts. Do you long for contact with Jesus who makes himself available as "God-with-us" and gives himself graciously to you in Eucharist?

December 24: Luke 1:67-79. "Blessed be the Lord God of Israel, / for he has looked favorably on his people and redeemed them." Read the whole canticle. Do you long for the Savior described here? What about Jesus most arouses your desire to be close to him?

Living This Week's Gospels

As Christian: Put in a visible place something that reminds you of the Great Commandment: "You shall love the Lord your God with all your heart..." (Matthew 22:37). It might be just the word "all."

As Disciple: Each time you see or hear something designed to arouse desire in you (advertisements, commercials, for example), ask yourself how real, how total is fulfillment which the satisfaction of this desire can give.

As Prophet: This week, as a gesture (which need be recognized only by yourself), give up something you have come to take for granted as necessary in your life.

As Priest: Each day this week make an act of deep adoration of God. You might kneel and kiss the floor each morning when you wake.

As King: Make a list of the priorities where you work, or in your family. What is the highest? Where is God?

CHRISTMAS
SEASON

Christmas Vigil

Glory and Praise

Isaiah 9:1-6; Titus 2:11-14; Luke 2:1-14

T he Christmas readings take us to the source of the hymn we proclaim at the beginning of our Eucharistic celebrations: "Glory to God in the highest, and peace to his people on earth." Every Sunday, except for Advent and Lent, we sing or recite the *Gloria*, "an ancient hymn in which the Church, assembled in the Spirit, praises and prays to the Father and the Lamb" *(General Instruction of the Roman Missal).*

Reciting the *Gloria* reminds us that we are an evangelized and evangelizing people. We have heard the Good News. We have recognized it as good—as more than good; it is the great light that shines now on the people who walked in darkness, and lived in the region and shadow of death. It is the news that the grace of God has appeared, the grace of our Lord Jesus Christ, bringing salvation to all.

For this day "a child has been born for us, / a son given to us; / authority rests upon his shoulders; / and he is named / Wonderful Counselor, Mighty God, / Everlasting Father, Prince of Peace." An angel tells the shepherds, "To you is born this day in the city of David a Savior, who is the Messiah, the Lord." Isaiah prophesied, "His authority shall grow continually, / and there shall be endless peace / for the throne of David and his kingdom. / He will establish and uphold it with justice and with righteousness / from this time onward and forevermore." We have something to sing about. Let us rejoice and be glad!

An evangelized people is a rejoicing people. And vice versa, people unable to rejoice have never been evangelized; they have never truly heard the Good News. But the Church has heard it, and the Church rejoices in it. We begin every

Eucharist proclaiming to one another that "the grace of our Lord Jesus Christ, the love of God, and communion in the Holy Spirit" are offered to us and to the world. If there are any who have never felt their "hearts burning within them" at the proclamation of this good news, they have not yet entered deeply enough into the life and joy of the Church.

A second sign that we have been evangelized is that we are evangelizers. Those who have heard the Good News cannot help proclaiming it. Those who know Jesus Christ share him with others, tell others about him, bring others to him. For two thousand years the Church has been doing this: in every country, town, parish and mission station throughout the world. In every place where Mass is celebrated, people hear the Good News read from Scripture; celebrate the Good News in community; offer Jesus Christ, the Good News incarnate, to the Father, and themselves with him, to bring his salvation, his light, his life to the world. And that is what we are doing today.

Every Mass is a new evangelization: a new discovery of the Good News of Christ, a new rejoicing in it, a new and deeper act of participating in the mystery of his presence and action in the world. At every Mass the angels are singing to us, "Glory to God in the highest, and on earth peace!" They are reminding us, "Do not be afraid. To you is born this day a Savior." John the Baptist is pointing him out to us again: "Here is the Lamb of God who takes away the sin of the world." God the Father is speaking from the cloud, "This is my Son, the Beloved, listen to him!" And the Church echoes, "Lord Jesus Christ, only Son of the Father, Lord God, Lamb of God, you take away the sin of the world: have mercy on us! Glory to God in the highest!"

Every Mass invites us to worship the Father, to give him thanks, to praise him for his glory. In every Mass we acknowledge that Jesus alone is the Holy One, Jesus alone is Lord, Jesus alone is the Most High, with the Holy Spirit, in the glory of God the Father. By saying "Amen!" we make him the foundation and goal of our lives. This is Christmas.

Reflecting on This Week's Gospels
December 26-31

Note: Holy Family Sunday (see page x) will replace one of these days. See below.

> *Pray daily: Jesus, help us to live as one holy family on earth, united with all people in respect and love. Let us experience now the joy and peace of our home with you in heaven. We ask this through your victory as Christ our Lord.*

December 26 (Saint Stephen). Matthew 10:17-22. "Brother will betray brother to death, and a father his child; children will rise against parents and have them put to death." If we have been made members of the Body of Christ and children of the Father by Baptism (and if some become this by Baptism of desire), whom can we kill who is not our brother or sister? Does this put all killing under a different light?

December 27 (Saint John): John 20:2-8. "Then the other disciple [John], who reached the tomb first, also went in, and he saw and believed." When you see another member of the Body of Christ, do you believe that Jesus is present and living in that person? How do you express this belief?

December 28 (Holy Innocents). Matthew 2:13-18. "When Herod saw that he had been tricked by the wise men, he was infuriated and he sent and killed all the [male] children in and around Bethlehem who were two years old or under...." In every war we sacrifice babies to preserve our "national security." Do we really differ from Herod?

December 29 (Fifth Day in Octave of Christmas): Luke 2:22-35. When Mary and Joseph brought in the child Jesus, Simeon blessed God, saying: "[M]y eyes have seen your salvation." Do you spontaneously bless God for his presence and action in every person? Or do you see some as adversaries or a threat to you? What is the answer to this?

December 30 (Sixth Day in Octave of Christmas):
Luke 2:36-40. "Anna began to praise God and to speak about the child to all who were looking for the redemption of Jerusalem." Do you please God when you recognize grace at work in others and speak of it?

December 31 (Seventh Day in Octave of Christmas):
John 1:1-18. "The light shines in the darkness, and the darkness did not overcome it." Can you affirm this with faith about every person who is still alive? In every human encounter, how can you keep yourself aware of the active presence and power of God?

Living This Week's Gospels

As Christian: Just as you consciously gave yourself to Christ by accepting your Baptism, so give yourself consciously to accepting every person on earth as family.

As Disciple: Read Ephesians 5:21 to 6:9, asking what general principle or truth all of this advice is based on. How can you apply Paul's suggestions to your own situation?

As Prophet: Ask systematically what special light of revelation shines in each of your friends or coworkers—and in yourself.

As Priest: Notice the pain of people you know or work with and join yourself to them as fellow-priest in offering it to God as part of Christ's redeeming sacrifice on earth.

As King: Recognize the ways in which grace is at work and winning (or making progress!) in various people you know, including those you do not like. Take each person into your heart as Simeon took Jesus into his arms, and praise God for his glory in each one. Do the same for yourself!

Holy Family Sunday

Portrait of a Family:
Blessed Are the Merciful

Sirach 3:2-6, 12-14; Colossians 3:12-21; Luke 2:22-40

It seems strange to us that a woman would have to be "purified" after childbirth; even stranger, perhaps, that the reason behind this Jewish law was the fact that birth involves the shedding of blood (see Leviticus 12, 1-8).

Isn't it true, however, that blood is always a sign to us that something is wrong? We associate blood with sickness, pain and death—none of which God wanted in his world (see Genesis 3:16-19; Romans 5:12 to 6:23). It is reasonable, then, that whenever blood becomes visible (or hurt, or sin, or death), God would require some visible act of response on our part to "make sense" out of what does not make sense: to integrate into the universe something that does not belong there. And what is it that gives a value, a role in human life to blood and pain? It is sacrifice. In her blood a woman gives life to a child. In his blood Jesus gave life to the world. Through our blood—the sacrifices we make in love—we give life to one another.

Did God require a ritual sacrifice every time blood was shed in order to teach us that blood and pain are purified of meaninglessness only through sacrifice? The pain we transform into love becomes the wine of the wedding feast. The "hour" of our redemption is the moment when blood is poured out as wine, and the wine is a pledge of love (see John 2: 1-11).

This is how priesthood and marriage are one: they are both dedications to giving life through the offering of ourselves. This offering has as its goal the formation of communities of grace. Matrimony is a consecration to forming Christian community in the home; Holy Orders on the level of the local Church. Together they are the sign that the world can be redeemed if we radically offer ourselves to be united in love.

Today's Gospel story combines two themes: purification from blood and the presentation/consecration of a firstborn child to God. Because God delivered the Jews from slavery by sacrificing every firstborn son in Egypt, every firstborn male in Israel belonged to God and had to be "bought back." This was done in two ways: by an offering, and by the consecration of the Levites (Numbers 18:16, 8:16). Of them God said, "I have taken them for myself in place of every firstborn." The tribe of Levi, then, was "sacrificed" ("made sacred," set aside) for priestly service as a sign that they were taken by God in place of firstborn sons.

In Jesus, both themes come together. As firstborn he was consecrated for our redemption (see 1 Corinthians 15:20 ff. and John 17:19). As Priest he overcame sin and death by offering his blood on the cross as the wine of the wedding feast to bring the world together into unity in love.

The Church combines both themes, not only in this one Gospel story, but by celebrating the Purification of Mary and the Presentation of Jesus as one feast (February 2). And by selecting this Gospel for the feast of the Holy Family, the Church calls our attention to the connection there is between the same two themes in family life. Every Christian family is a community of people consecrated to the Lord as priests and dedicated to redeeming the whole human race through the offering of themselves—of their blood and pain and sacrifices—in love.

The Levites were offered in place of the firstborn of Israel only. But every Christian baptized into the priesthood of Christ is offered, as Jesus was, to "buy back" every other member of the human race. And the way we live out this offering is by trying to bring about that community—that oneness of all people with each other and with God—which Jesus came to accomplish (see Ephesians 1:10). Christian families exist not just to take care of one another, but to offer, to "sacrifice" themselves to bring about unity in the whole human race. When Jesus teaches, "Blessed are the merciful" (those who help others out of a sense of relatedness), he is calling us to be one family on earth: to consecrate and offer ourselves for this.

Note: The weekly readings for the feast of the Holy Family, if it falls on a Sunday, are the readings for the weekdays within the Octave of Christmas (above) because the Holy Family is normally celebrated on the Sunday within the week that follows Christmas.

"Mother of God"

Numbers 6:22-27; Galatians. 4:4-7; Luke 2:16-21

W hy do we call Mary the "Mother of God"? This title is not in Scripture. It was defined as a dogma of faith at the Council of Ephesus in the year A.D. 431. Before that date the title was widely used in the Church but there was debate about it.

Why would anyone debate it? It is clear in Scripture that Mary was the mother of Jesus, and that Jesus is God. So why not call her God's mother?

The answer touches the core of Christianity itself. That is why there was so much argument about it. The Church did not give Mary this title to glorify her. As much as we love Mary, the Church teaches nothing about Mary just to honor her. All the Church's doctrines about Mary were defined for the sake of saying something about Jesus or about the mystery and gift of redemption. We teach about Mary in order to understand Jesus and to understand ourselves as the Church, the body of Jesus redeemed by his grace.

What is at issue here? Why is it so important to insist that Mary should be called "Mother of God?" Why not just say she is the "mother of Jesus" or the "mother of Jesus' body," and sidestep all the questions that come up when you say that a creature is the mother of the God who created her and who existed before she did?

In a nutshell, the Church insists on this title in order to avoid dividing Jesus. To say that Mary is the mother of Jesus' humanity, but not of his divinity, is to give the impression that there were two separate, independent parts in Jesus: a human part and a divine part, and that these were not really united as one in a single person. Similarly, to say that Mary is only the mother of Jesus' body, is to divide Jesus' body from his soul. By insisting that Mary is the "Mother of God," the Church is refusing to accept any division in Jesus. He is all that he is: fully human and fully divine.

But wouldn't it be true to say that all mothers are only the mother of the body? Every time a baby is conceived, God has to create the soul, since a spiritual soul—intellect and free will—cannot be explained by the joining of two material cells. Every time conception takes place through a man's and a woman's expression of love, God is present, joining his love to theirs, expressing his love in and through theirs, breathing in the soul in his personal act of love, saying again as he said on the first day of creation, with a love we cannot imagine, "Let it be!" (See Genesis 1.)

This is true. But we do not say of our own mothers that they are just the "mother of our bodies." Parenthood is relationship to a person, to everything that person is. And what our own fathers and mothers are to us, Mary is to Jesus: She is the mother of the person, Jesus Christ. And that person is God. So we call Mary "Mother of God" to make the point that Jesus is not divided into two separate beings. Jesus is one person, the Second Person of the Blessed Trinity, existing in two natures: one human, one divine, which are made one in the unity of his life as the person named Jesus Christ.

When we refuse to separate the humanity of Jesus from his divinity, we lay the foundation for refusing to separate Jesus from his body, the Church—or the divine work of Jesus from the human work of the Church. In the Church, Jesus shares his own divine life with the members of his body, and he shares in their human lives—as the water and the wine take on one common taste at Mass. In the Church Jesus lives and works in his members, humanly and divinely; and the members live and work in Jesus, humanly and divinely. When we say that Mary is the "Mother of God" it helps us realize the mystery we are proclaiming when we say with Saint Paul that we are the "body of Christ."

Reflecting on This Week's Gospels

January 2-7

Pray daily: Lord, you chose Mary to be the Mother of God. You have chosen me to be your body on earth. Teach me to accept the mystery of my being and to live as your embodied presence on earth.

January 2: John 1:19-28. "This is the testimony given by John when the Jews sent priests and Levites from Jerusalem to ask him, 'Who are you?' he confessed and did not deny it, but confessed, 'I am not the Messiah.'" Would you answer in the same way? Is Jesus continuing his work as Messiah in you? How?

January 3: John 1:29-34. John said, "[T]he one who sent me to baptize with water said to me, 'He on whom you see the Spirit descend and remain is the one who baptizes with the Holy Spirit.'" Has the Holy Spirit come down on you? Does he remain with you? How does the power of the Spirit show itself in what you do?

January 4: Wednesday: John 1:35-42. "Andrew first found his brother Simon and said to him, 'We have found the Messiah' (which is translated Anointed). He brought Simon to Jesus, who looked at him and said, 'You are Simon, son of John. You are to be called Cephas' (which is translated Peter)." When were you first brought to Jesus? What did he say to you? Did he give you a name? A mission? What is it?

January 5: John 1:43-51. Nathanael said to Philip, "Can anything good come out of Nazareth?" Philip said to him, "Come and see." Do you think anything good can come of you? How good? Why?

January 6: Mark 1:7-11. This is what John proclaimed: "One who is more powerful than I is coming after me. I am not worthy to stoop down and untie the thongs of his sandals. I have baptized you with water; he will baptize you with the Holy Spirit." When were you baptized with the Holy Spirit?

What effect did it have on you? How is that visible in your life?

January 7: John 2:1-12. "Jesus did this [changed the water into wine], the first of his signs, in Cana of Galilee, and revealed his glory; and his disciples believed in him." How did this particular miracle "reveal Jesus' glory"? What kind of transformations is he working on earth today? What transformation has he worked in you?

Living This Week's Gospels

As Christian: See how you feel saying to yourself, "I am the body of Christ. I am the embodied presence of Jesus in the world."

As Disciple: Read Romans, chapter 12. Relate what you read to yourself.

As Prophet: Examine your room, your home, your workplace. Is there anything visible that is unworthy of the body of Christ?

As Priest: At the Eucharist, offer yourself in Christ and with Christ as his Body. Think of what it means to be offered with him as a "living sacrifice" for the life of the world in everything you do all day.

As King: Notice the living conditions in the parts of town you drive through. Are they worthy of the body of Christ? What about the environment where you work? What do you see in your city which is unworthy of the body of Christ? What can you do about it?

Epiphany

The Path to Light:
Blessed Are the Pure in Heart

Isaiah 60:1-6; Ephesians 3:2-3, 5-6; Matthew 2:1-12

W hat is the key to the "experience of God?" Why does God seem very real to some people and not at all to others? Why can some people see that the teaching of Jesus is true, while others cannot see it at all?

Why is it that some people find Mass a source of comfort, of clarity and strength, while others just suffer through it bored? Why is the sacrament of Reconciliation such a tremendous help to some Catholics, while others have to force themselves just to go to confession once or twice a year? Why are some people drawn to pray while others hardly ever think of praying?

It is not a matter of brains or of education. There have been saints and mystics among the most brilliant and the least intelligent of people, and among the most and the least educated. Nor is it just chance, or the fact of having been born into a religious environment. Frequently the children of very religious parents grow up never experiencing real, personal faith, while out of the most corrupt families saints have sprouted like roses out of a dunghill.

Today's Gospel is a good example of the problem: who would be less likely to recognize and experience Jesus Christ than a group of pagan stargazers who were both geographically and culturally remote from the People of God? Why did they have the faith to accept Jesus absolutely—no ifs, ands or buts; just, "We have come to adore him!"—while Herod wanted only to protect his own position?

Jesus gives us a key when he says, "Blessed are the pure in heart, for they will see God." What best prepares and enables us to "see" the truths of faith, to recognize God's action in our lives, and to hear his voice is not a particular type of personality or some kind of cultural predisposition. Nor is it training and technique. It is the simple fact of being pure in heart, undivided in desire.

To be pure in heart does not mean that we choose, theoretically, to give God first place in our lives, but just barely. In that kind if situation there is a lot of interior division and conflict. Our hearts are torn between a chosen, deliberate desire to be on good terms with God and other desires—which are also deliberately embraced and chosen—for many other things we have targeted to pursue for their own sakes, quite apart from any relationship they may or may not have with God. If we are set on having the best of both worlds, or even a sixty-forty split, we are not pure in heart. We are divided. And this is an obstacle to seeing the truths of faith and experiencing God's action in our lives.

The pure in heart may feel the same desire for the things and experiences of this world that anyone feels. The difference is that they have refused to embrace any of these desires, or to make any one of them active as a working motivation in their lives except in the measure that they believe the desire will lead them into a better relationship with God.

Any felt desire is in itself just a fact; not an engagement of the will in any particular direction. The desire to own or enjoy something, to succeed in some line of work, to escape pain, to enter into an intimate relationship of love with someone, or to get revenge against someone—all these are in themselves just facts, just feelings or desires. They do not make us better or worse as persons, because they are not personal choices until we stamp them "approved" or "disapproved" with our wills. When we do this we activate them as driving forces for action. We make them "our" desires.

Those who radically choose to pursue nothing except what they perceive as helping them to love and serve God, these are the ones who "see" God in this life. For them the reality of God and the value of religion are matters of experience, an epiphany. They follow one star, and it leads them to Jesus Christ.

Reflecting on This Week's Gospels

Week after Epiphany

Pray daily: Thy blessed birth, O Jesus, Christ our Lord, has lifted up for the world the light of holy wisdom. For on this day the Magi, who revered the star, by the true light were enlightened. Thee to adore, the holy Sun of Justice coming from above; and to behold Thee, the rising Dawn of truth and love. Glory to thee, O Lord.

Monday: Matthew 4:12-17, 23-25. "The people who sat in darkness have seen a great light." What is the darkness? What is the light? How have you shone as a star in the night?

Tuesday: Mark 6:34-44. Jesus said to the apostles in reply, "You give them something to eat." "How can I, Lord? I have nothing to share!" "You yourself will be filled by the witness you bear." How have you experienced this?

Wednesday: Mark 6:45-52. "But when they saw him walking on the sea, they thought it was a ghost and cried out...." If we cry out together in the shadow of death, the waves will be stilled by his answering breath. How often do you join yourself to others in praying for needs? Is there a difference?

Thursday: Luke 4:14-22. "When he came to Nazareth, where he had been brought up, he went to the synagogue on the sabbath day, as was his custom." If the Light of the world had just worshipped alone, none of his brilliance on us would have shone. How do you share your light during liturgy?

Friday: Luke 5:12-16. "[M]any crowds would gather to hear him and to be cured of their diseases. But he would withdraw to deserted places and pray." If the light is not nurtured in silence and prayer, the power to heal will soon not be there. How much time do you spend on Scripture alone? How much with others?

Saturday: John 3:22-30. John the Baptist said: "The friend of the bridegroom, who stands and hears him, rejoices greatly at the bridegroom's voice. For this reason my joy has been fulfilled." The joy of the bridegroom, the flush of the bride: Epiphany!—Signs of the Spirit inside. How does my joy in God appear?

Living This Week's Gospels

As Christian: Make a list of the "stars" from the culture which have guided your path. Which have guided you into "the way of peace"? Which have not?

As Disciple: After encountering Jesus the Magi returned to their country "by a different path." What can you change in your life-style which will make manifest that your encounters with Jesus have changed your course?

As Prophet: Make a list of the "stars" you have recognized as coming from God in your life and followed? Where did they lead you?

As Priest: Decide each day on one gift to offer to Jesus which is worthy of you.

As King: Ask what there is in your life that you control, which you can redirect more effectively into "the way of peace" by following Christ's teaching.

ORDINARY TIME

First Sunday of
the Year
Through
Ninth Sunday of
the Year

The Sign of Divinity: Blessed Are the Peacemakers

Isaiah 42:1-4, 6-7; Acts 10:34-38; Mark 1:7-11

John proclaimed that the One he announced was so much more powerful than he, that he was not even worthy to undo his sandal straps. We know that Jesus was in fact God himself, and that by "baptizing us in the Holy Spirit" he would make us divine ourselves.

If we find this hard to believe or grasp, how should we think Jesus felt, having heard from his mother that he was the Messiah promised by God and seeing nothing happening in his life that would confirm this?

Jesus saw no sign in his life which he or any other Jew could have recognized as a clue that he was the Messiah. No prophet had been sent to anoint him as Samuel anointed David (1 Samuel 16), and John, who was announcing the Messiah, did not even know who the Messiah was (John 1:31-34). Jesus had no money, no influence, no followers, no army, no power—not even any power from God that he knew about—and no instructions about how he was to set about saving the world. He had nothing except his mother's account of the events of his conception and birth. And after these, thirty years of nothing!

Then came his Baptism and the Father's voice saying, "You are my beloved Son." And that was all. No visible endowment with power; no instructions; no acclamation by the people begging him to lead them. Jesus still looked like an ordinary carpenter's son and still felt just as clueless about how to save the world.

This may be the key to what the Father was doing. He left Jesus without any of the signs a Jew would recognize as identifying the Messiah, because the kind of Savior everyone expected was not the kind Jesus was to be. He was not to save the world by establishing a political kingdom of justice and prosperity. He was not to stamp out the opposition by military might enhanced by God's supporting power. He was not to triumph over his enemies in any recognizable way during his lifetime. On the contrary, he was to use no weapon but his words, no power but the power of truth, of healing and of love. He would die abused and defeated, without God lifting a finger to save him. To all appearances evil would triumph over Jesus as it always seems to do, by crushing the weak with arrogant physical force.

And this, contrary to what anyone would have expected, was the real sign that Jesus was indeed the Son of God. If Jesus had saved us in the way we expected; if God had been predictable, we would have reason to ask whether he was indeed God or a projection of our minds. A Zen riddle says, "If you meet the Buddha on the road, kill him!" The real God, the God who is, is not a God we should expect to recognize!

The mystery of redemption is that the way of salvation Jesus taught and modeled for us during his life is something we humans steadfastly refuse to accept or recognize as salvation. The fact is, Jesus saved us by simply enduring evil—injustice, violence, even death—and loving back. To accept him as Savior is to accept that the way of salvation consists in enduring evil and loving back. The way to peace is to respond to violence with peace.

We, however, in response to aggression do what Jesus refused to do, to protect either himself or others: We resort to violence. We fight back. We go to war. We kill. We seek to save our lives in this world, which Jesus warned us is the way to lose ourselves (see Matthew 16:24-26). In spite of his teaching and example we cling to the belief that it is really power and force, not love, which save us.

Jesus showed himself Son of God by saving the world not by force, but through gentleness and love. And he said that the same sign will identify those who have received from him the gift of divine life: "Blessed are the peacemakers, for they will be called children of God."

Reflecting on This Week's Gospels

First Week of the Year

Pray daily: Lord, I believe that you are the Savior of the world. Help me to believe that your way is the way to fulfillment; that your truth leads to freedom; that the life you give is worth the sacrifice of life itself in love.

Monday: Mark 1:14-20. "Now after John was arrested, Jesus came to Galilee proclaiming the Good News of God, and saying, 'The time is fulfilled, and the kingdom of God has come near; repent and believe in the good news.'" What motive does Jesus give you for changing your mind about the way you live?

Tuesday: Mark 1:21-28. "They were astonished at his teaching, for he taught them as one having authority, and not as the scribes." Who are the "teachers" of attitudes and values in our culture? What authority do they claim?

Wednesday: Mark 1:29-39. He told them, "Let us go on to the neighboring towns, so that I may proclaim the message there also; for that is what I came out to do." What did Jesus see as more important in his ministry: healing miracles or teaching? Which do you use him for today?

Thursday. Mark 1:40-45. A leper came to him, begged him and said, "If you choose, you can make me clean." Moved with pity, Jesus stretched out his hand and touched him, saying, "I do choose. Be made clean!" Do you believe Jesus really wants to give you everything that is for your good? For what do you ask him consistently?

Friday: Mark 2:1-2. When it became known that Jesus was in Capernaum, many gathered together so that there was no longer room for them, not even around the door, and he preached the word to them. When, where, through whom does Jesus preach and teach today? Do you go to listen every chance you get?

Saturday: Mark 2:13-17. "As he was walking along, he saw Levi, son of Alphaeus, sitting at the tax booth and he said to him, 'Follow me.'" And he got up and followed him." Have you experienced this same call personally? When? How? How are you responding?

Living This Week's Gospels

As Christian: Notice how many people, things, techniques, ideas you put trust in daily. Try to match each one with an act of trust in Christ.

As Disciple: List all the sources of information or advice you use as a guide for daily decisions. Work at making the words and example of Jesus a factor in each choice.

As Prophet: Decide on one way each day that you will use Christ's way of love, gentleness and persuasion rather than power or threats to accomplish your goals.

As Priest: Each day find one way, no matter how small, to sacrifice yourself in love for others in union with the Lamb of God, who gave himself for the life of the world.

As King: Set out to change something in your environment —at home, at work, in your social or civic life—by using only the power of truth and love. Repeat constantly in your heart, in every circumstance, "Thy kingdom come!"

The Fundamental Question: Blessed Are the Persecuted

1 Samuel 3:3-10, 19; 1 Corinthians 6:13-15, 17-20;
John 1:35-42

Once John pointed Jesus out to his hearers, their lives could never be the same. They had to make a fundamental decision: to accept Jesus as the Messiah on John's testimony or to reject him. From those who accepted John's testimony enough to investigate further, Jesus required a further decision: "What are you looking for?" he asked. What kind of Messiah do you want? What kind will you accept?

The answer they blurted out was more of an answer than they knew. "Rabbi," they said—and the Gospel takes care to point out that this means "Teacher"—"Where do you live?" The one they were actually looking for, whether they knew it yet or not, was Jesus. Where he was, there the Messiah would be. And in calling him "Teacher" they already identified the kind of Messiah he would be. Insofar as his human actions were concerned, he would save the world by word and example, by being a teacher, the Teacher of life. And the core of Jesus' teaching about how to live in this world is given in the Baptist's introduction of him: "Look, here is the Lamb of God!"

The lamb is a symbol of gentleness and vulnerability. In Scripture, the lamb is the victim who is offered by Abraham (Genesis 22: 7-8) and by Moses (Exodus 12); and for atonement (Leviticus 12:6-8; 23:27 and Numbers 29:7-8). In calling Jesus "Lamb of God," John identifies him with the "Suffering Servant," who is described as a lamb led to slaughter (Isaiah 53:7). And at Jesus' Baptism in the Jordan, God the Father made the same identification (Matthew

3:16-17 and Isaiah 11:2, 42:1). In the Aramaic that John
the Baptist would have been speaking, the same phrase can
mean either "servant of God" or "lamb of God"
(see *The Jerome Biblical Commentary*).

Since this identification is made by John the Baptist at
Jesus' Baptism, we can take it that when we are baptized
"into Christ," we not only become beloved children of the
Father as "sons in the Son," but also one with Jesus as
Suffering Servant; that is, our Baptism commits us to accept
also for ourselves the role, the values and that particular use
(i.e., non-use) of power that are manifested symbolically by
the figure of the lamb and revealed in the flesh by Jesus the
Suffering Servant. In other words, "what we are looking for"
in Jesus as Messiah is not a victorious ruler, but one who
saves the world by teaching us to endure evil with love and
to give up our lives like sacrificial lambs so that others might
come into the truth and live.

The Eucharist also commits us to this. In the Eastern
Church the bread of Eucharist is called "lamb." And in our
Latin rite Jesus is proclaimed "Lamb of God" four times
before communion. Saint Augustine instructs us, "Be what
you consume and consume what you are" at communion. To
receive Jesus as "Lamb of God" is to accept for ourselves the
salvation he offered—which is a salvation found through
accepting to lose our lives, to be led as lambs to the
slaughter—and it is to commit ourselves to the work of
saving the world as he did: by enduring evil with love,
turning the other cheek, and praying with love for those who
persecute us, oppress us and violate our rights (see Matthew
5:38-48). Identified with the Lamb of God, we must never
pay back evil with evil, but rather seek to be a blessing to
those who do us harm (see Romans 12:17; 1 Thessalonians
5:15). As Jesus saved us by letting himself be led as a lamb
to the slaughter, so we are called to save others by returning
good for evil, even to the witness of our blood (see 1 Peter
1:18 to 4:19).

The comfort of this teaching is not in any promise of
security or peace on earth, but in the assurance that this is

Christ's way and the only way to save ourselves and this world from evil. Self-sacrifice, not self-defense, is our salvation. Love, not power, preserves us. The fundamental question is: Are we willing to accept this kind of salvation and Jesus as this kind of Savior?

Reflecting on This Week's Gospels

Second Week of the Year

> ***Pray daily:*** *Lord Jesus, you came to earth to excite our desire. Inflame my mind with desire for your truth, my heart with desire for intimate union with you, my will with zeal to do your work on earth.*

Monday: Mark 2:18-22. "No one puts new wine into old wineskins...but one puts new wine into fresh wineskins." To receive the "new teaching" of Jesus, what assumptions and structures of your life-style do you need to call into question?

Tuesday: Mark 2:23-28. Jesus said, "The sabbath was made for humankind, not humankind for the sabbath." Why did God give us the sabbath rest we observe on Sunday? Do you use it for that?

Wednesday: Mark 3:1-6. Then he said to them, "Is it lawful to do good or to do harm on the sabbath, to save life or to kill?" All God's laws are life-enhancing. Do you see every sin as a diminishment of your life and that of others?

Thursday: Mark 3:7-12. He had cured many and, as a result, those who had diseases were pressing upon him to touch him. Do you see anything Jesus has done for other people? How does this move you to get closer to him yourself?

Friday: Mark 3:13-19. He appointed twelve [apostles] that they might be with him and he might send them forth to preach. Would you have wanted to be chosen for this? To "leave everything" and then be with Jesus constantly? To be sent out by him? Is your answer a key to whether you seek intimacy with him now? To your zeal in doing his work?

Saturday: Mark 3:20-21. The crowd gathered, making it impossible for Jesus and the apostles to eat. When his relatives heard of this they set out to seize him, for they said, "He is out of his mind." Has anything you have done for Jesus, for others, ever made people think you were out of your mind? What should you think of this?

Living This Week's Gospels

As Christian: Put something in sight that reminds you of Jesus all day: at work, in your car, at home, in social life. It can be a medal, picture or some symbol which only you can recognize.

As Disciple: Read at least one line of Scripture every day on waking and before going to sleep.

As Prophet: Each day choose to do some action which expresses response to what you have read in Scripture. Learn in order to do.

As Priest: Make the sign of the cross on some part of your body every morning, consecrating that function (for example, lips for speech, hands for work) to be used as Christ's body to give his life, his healing to others.

As King: Each time you have an angry thought which inclines you to violence in word or act, try to invent an alternate way in which you could respond to the situation— one which follows Christ's principle of renewing society by converting hearts through love and truth rather than through force and retaliation.

A Community Focus

Jonah 3:1-5, 10; 1 Corinthians 7:29-31; Mark 1:14-20

There is a contrast between the "call to repentance" (to a change of mind, heart, direction) in Jonah and in the Gospel. The reason Jonah gives is, "Forty days more, and Nineveh shall be overthrown." In other words, "Something bad is about to happen: change direction or else!" In the Gospel, however, the reason Jesus preaches is, "This is the time of fulfillment. The reign of God is at hand!" Jesus is saying, "Something great is happening! Change direction or lose out!"

This pinpoints as well as anything the change that has taken place in Church preaching since Vatican II. The emphasis used to be on keeping the law of God out of fear: "Do what God says or else!" The focus of morality was on those things which were considered "mortal sin"—that is, acts so evil in themselves that to do them was to condemn oneself to everlasting punishment in hell—forever and ever.

This approach seemed to work. Perhaps it really did not, but one had the impression in those days that anybody who went to church was pretty concerned about "mortal sin." People fell into a lot of things which were preached as mortal sin, but they worried about it. And they tried to get to the Sacrament of Reconciliation and back into God's good graces as soon as they could. The "or else" of everlasting hell was something to take seriously. It still is!

What has changed? What has not changed? We still believe that anyone who commits "mortal sin" is choosing to do something so seriously incompatible with being Christ's Body on earth, so contrary to the way of life he taught and to the divine life we are called to live, that the choice to commit "mortal sin" is in fact a decision to give up the life of grace, to give up union with Christ, to stop trying to live as a child of God, a temple of the Holy Spirit, a coworker with Jesus in the mission of redeeming the world. And to give up union with Christ on this earth is to give up everlasting union with him in heaven. It is to trade heaven for hell. That teaching has not changed.

What has changed? For one thing, the Church recognizes that theologians were too quick to agree on what actions were serious enough to be "mortal sin." To miss Mass one Sunday would send you to hell as surely as committing murder would. And since missing Mass was a more common temptation than murder, priests preached on it more. The result was that Catholics were more concerned about missing Mass than they were, for example, about whom they killed in war. By declaring so many things "mortal sin," teachers made us less able to recognize real evil when we saw it.

Also, by focusing our attention on avoiding hell (the "bad news") preachers turned our attention away from the Good News of the fulfillment offered by Jesus Christ. We were so intent on not doing what was "mortal" (deadly) that we hardly thought about what was life-giving. Catholics saw more value in "being there" at Mass—even distractedly, inertly, without entering into the celebration—than in reading Scripture attentively at home (not that this should be considered an either-or option, of course). It was more important not to eat meat on Friday than it was to receive the Bread of Life in Communion on any other day of the week. We were like people so concerned about not getting sick that we did not take care of our health!

The focus of preaching today is on the positive invitation to follow the teaching of Jesus into the fullness of life. Jesus offers everyone "life to the full" on this earth as well as in heaven. But we cannot enter into the fullness of life by avoiding sin; we have to positively learn from Jesus Christ and live his teachings "to the full." His words are the words of life, but only if we live them. That is why the focus today is on what we should do in order to grow in the life of grace rather than on what we should avoid just to "preserve" it.

Reflecting on This Week's Gospels

Third Week of the Year

Pray daily: Lord Jesus, you came that we might "have life, and have it to the full." Let this desire of yours fill my heart. Fill me with desire to open myself to your life and to share it with others.

Monday: Mark 3:22-30. "And if a house is divided against itself, that house will not be able to stand." In how many ways are you helped by your relationship *(koinonia)* with others in the parish? How do you help others?

Tuesday: Mark 3:31-35. Jesus said, "Here are my mother and my brothers. For whoever does the will of God is my brother and sister and mother." What kind of relationship do you want to have with Jesus? Servant? Follower? Friend? Family? Spouse? What are you willing to do to enter into a deeper, more intimate relationship with him?

Wednesday: Mark 4:1-20. Jesus said, "Other seed fell into good soil and brought forth grain, growing up and increasing and yielding thirty and sixty and a hundredfold." Why do seeds grow best in a garden? What makes a parish "rich soil" for God's word to grow? Is this true for me? Could it be more so?

Thursday: Mark 4:21-25. He also told them, "[T]he measure you give will be the measure you get." Is this true of the benefit we receive from membership (community) in a parish? How much do you give to/receive from others? Are they related?

Friday: Mark 4:26-34. The Kingdom of God "which, when sown upon the ground, is the smallest of all the seeds on earth; yet when it is sown it grows up and becomes the greatest of all shrubs and puts forth large branches, so that the birds of the air can make nests in its shade." What draws people to the Church? To the parish? How do you?

Saturday: Mark 4:35-41. Jesus was in the stern, asleep.... They woke him and said to him, "Teacher, do you not care that we are perishing?" Do you, as Christ's Body on earth, seem to be "asleep" to others' needs? Do you care that they are "perishing"?

Living This Week's Gospels

As Christian: For one week write down each night how your faith has enriched your life that day.

As Disciple: Each morning ask how the day's reading (on this page) shows you a way to grow in love for God and others.

As Prophet: Identify one thing that would change in your life if you asked, not just what is right or wrong, but what bears witness to (expresses) the teachings (the attitudes, values, goals) of Jesus.

As Priest: Think of one way of ministering to others which also causes you to grow in faith, in hope, or in love.

As King: In one activity of your day consciously change your focus: assume responsibility, not just for being moral and ethical, but for extending the reign of Christ. Afterwards, ask how this has affected your relationship with Jesus and with others.

Made One by the Word

Deuteronomy 18:15-20; 1 Corinthians 7:32-35; Mark 1:21-28

When Moses told the Jews God had promised "to raise up for you a prophet like me from among your own people," he was telling them God would hold them together as a people, through someone who would proclaim his word.

What united Israel was the word of God. They were identified as a people, united with one another, through the "common unity" of their faith in God's revelation, and through the communal response they made to God's words embodied in their laws and customs. Israel was not just a race or tribe; what made this people so special and their history so significant was the fact they were the chosen receptacle for God's word on earth and the instrument through which God acted for the redemption of the world. They needed prophets! The word of God had to be proclaimed in their midst for them to keep their identity and their dynamism.

When Jesus came, he was the Prophet of all prophets, the Word of God made flesh. To be united as a Church today we have to be united through the word of God embodied in the living person of Jesus—Jesus present, teaching and ministering in his Church, expressing himself through "word and sacrament." Only this can hold us together and give us identity and dynamism as the people of God.

Peter proclaimed Jesus the prophet Moses had promised, and at the same time warned, "Everyone who does not listen to that prophet will be cut off from the people." That is still true: If we do not positively listen, seek out, pay attention to the word of God proclaimed in the Church, we find ourselves cut off from the action, alienated from the community of the People of God. We may still come to Mass faithfully—well, consistently; not really *faithfully*—but we will be out of touch, not really able to enter into the ongoing life of the community. To really be an active, participating member of the people of God we have to be constantly, continuously formed by the word of God. We cannot even participate fully in the liturgy unless we know Scripture.

"Liturgy has always been impregnated by Holy Scripture: from it liturgy has borrowed its language and has nourished itself on its substance. The screen which separated people from the liturgy came not only from the Latin, but also from ignorance of the Scriptures.... Renewal of the liturgy is inseparable from a return to catechesis and preaching based on the Bible." (from Bernard Botte, *From Silence to Participation*).

When Jesus taught the people were "astonished..., for he taught them as one having authority and not as the scribes." Their spontaneous response was, "What is this? A new teaching with authority!"

The teaching of Jesus in the Church is always "new"— "ever ancient, ever new," as Saint Augustine said of God's love; or, in Jesus' words, it is a teaching which continuously offers "what is new and what is old" (see Matthew 13:52). The consistency of Church teaching with Scripture and with the past is what keeps us as Church from disintegrating; the newness of the Church's insights and application of the Scriptures to modern questions is what keeps us from stagnating.

Saint Paul's letter invites us to say the same thing about marriage—or any deep human relationship. Paul, speaking of marriage as he observed it, said that concern about "pleasing one's wife or husband" distracted spouses from focusing on God. But a relationship based on finding God in each other and on seeking union with each other through common reflection on God's word would make "pleasing God" and pleasing each other one and the same thing. Every Christian relationship should be based on listening together to the word of God.

Reflecting on This Week's Gospels

Fourth Week of the Year

Pray daily: Lord Jesus, you gave us your word to
unite us in mind and heart to you and to each other.
Give us the faith to read your word, to reflect on it
and share it with one another, that we all may be one
in love.

Monday: Mark 5:1-20. The man had been dwelling among
the tombs.... Night and day he was crying out and bruising
himself with stones. How many people isolate and keep
damaging themselves by sin? What can you do about it?

Tuesday: Mark 5:21-43. She said, "If I but touch his
clothes, I will be made well." What could you cure in
yourself by contact with Christ? By reflecting on his words?

Wednesday: Presentation. Luke 2:22-40. Simeon blessed
God, saying. "Now, Master, you may let your servant go in
peace, according to your word, for my eyes have seen your
salvation." What words of God have you seen fulfilled in
your life? How often do you reflect on his promises?

Thursday: Mark 6:7-13. He summoned the Twelve and
began to send them out two by two and gave them authority
over unclean spirits. Do you believe that, united with others
in prayer and ministry, you have power to heal and to free
people from the power of evil? How does God's word unite
you to others?

Friday: Mark 6:14-29. Herod feared John, knowing him to
be a righteous and holy man, and he protected him. When he
heard him speak he was very much perplexed, yet he liked to
listen to him. Have you experienced the attraction that the
word of God has even for people who resist it? How often do
you quote God's word to others?

Saturday: Mark 6:30-34. When he disembarked and saw
the vast crowd, his heart was moved with pity for them, for

"they were like sheep without a shepherd; and he began to teach them many things." How does teaching gather together those "without a shepherd"? How can you help this happen?

Living This Week's Gospels

As Christian: Each time you are tempted in any way, say to yourself, "the truth shall make you free." Then try to think of some word of Christ that applies to the situation.

As Disciple: Identify some specific issues that divide you from others. Read a few lines of Scripture each day, looking for something that will help you seek union.

As Prophet: Each time this week that you hear anything said that is divisive, say something that leads to understanding or openness toward others.

As Priest: Jesus quoted Scripture frequently to help people. Do it once this week with a friend or someone who believes in him.

As King: Post where you can see it some word of Jesus which encourages you to keep trying to change the world (for example, John 16:33).

Fifth Sunday of the Year

The Cost of Contribution

Job 7:1-4, 6-7; 1 Corinthians 9:16-19, 22-23; Mark 1:29-39

Job expresses well the way most people feel some days and many people feel every day: that human life is a "drudgery," the uninspired and uninspiring daily treadmill of just working for a living (as opposed to living for a work), motivated by no higher value than necessity. This is the service of a slave: empty days, nights that are a relief from nothing, and a death "without hope" that closes nothingness with nothing.

By contrast, Paul says that his recompense for proclaiming the Gospel is that he is able to do it "free of charge." He specifically does not work for money, which keeps him conscious that the work itself is what inspires him, motivates him and fulfills him. He says more precisely later on that what "impels" him, "urges him on," is "the love of Christ.... He died for all, so that those who live might live no longer for themselves but for him" (2 Corinthians 5:14-15).

This is the meaning in life we claim for all the members of Christ's body during the Eucharistic Prayer of the Mass: "[H]e destroyed death and restored life. And that we might live no longer for ourselves but for him, he sent the Holy Spirit from you, Father, as his first gift to those who believe, to complete his work on earth and bring us the fullness of grace."

Paul's motive (and ours) for getting up in the morning is love: love of God and love for other people. We are not slaves to any necessity imposed on us by society but, like Paul, we have freely made ourselves "slaves to all" so that Christ might use us to give "life to the full" to all who accept to grow by his grace into intimate union with God.

The Gospel challenges us to believe that we have the

power to be a healing community—a Church in whom
Jesus is still curing the sick, preaching the good news and
expelling demons, not just of Galilee, but of the world. If we
are a Church (an *ecclesia*, an "assembly," a community of
people) who truly live "no longer for ourselves but for him"
and for his people, then Jesus who lives in us will be free to
continue in us his mission of healing and saving the world.
And that will be our reason for getting up in the morning.

To enable us to live "no longer for ourselves but for him"
and his people, God has sent the Holy Spirit as his first gift
to those who believe, to complete his work on earth and
bring us the fullness of grace. It is through union with,
surrender to, the Spirit of God within us that we are able to
heal the woundedness around us, overcome the power of evil
wherever we encounter it ("expel demons") and by our own
presence and action "proclaim the good news" of Christ's
continuing presence and activity in the world. Healing and
saving the world is not something we can do by our own
power; it is through the power of the Spirit who has been
given to us. But we must do something to let that power
work through us.

The first thing we must do is desire it. Do we truly,
deeply, passionately desire to "live now, no longer for
ourselves but for him"? Have we become convinced that
the only way to "save our lives on this earth"—to find the
fullness of meaning, value and joy in life—is to "lose" them
in love and service to others as members of Christ's saving
body? Or do we still settle for the cheap happiness we can
find in focusing on our own desires and satisfaction?

The second requirement for letting the power of the
Spirit work through us is discipleship. If we are not a
community of people immersed in remembrance of and
reflection on God's word, we will not have the vocabulary
to understand the Spirit's voice. The cost of being a healing,
life-giving Church is the investment of time in learning
from Jesus Christ.

Reflecting on This Week's Gospels

Fifth Week of the Year

*Pray daily: Lord, you have called me to live no
longer for myself, but for you and for others in love.
Give me a hunger for your word, so that my heart
may be transformed.*

Monday: Mark 6:53-56. "And wherever he went, into
villages or cities or farms, they laid the sick in the
marketplaces, and begged him that they might touch even
the fringe of his cloak; and all who touched it were healed."
When, how, does Jesus have this healing effect today?

Tuesday: Mark 7:1-13. Jesus said, "Isaiah prophesied
rightly about you hypocrites, as it is written, 'This people
honors me with their lips, / but their hearts are far from me.'"
How can you make all the words of the Mass, of the
Scriptures that are read, words that resonate in your heart,
words that move you?

Wednesday: Mark 7:14-23. Jesus said "Listen to me, all of
you, and understand: there is nothing outside a person that
by going in can defile, but the things that come out are what
defile." Jesus is talking about foods; but can words or images
"from outside" defile me? How? Can God's words purify
me? How?

Thursday: Mark 7:24-30. "Sir, even the dogs under the
table eat the children's crumbs." Jesus said, "[T]he demon
has left your daughter." Do you see Jesus as this woman did?
Do you pounce on every chance to hear his word? Do you
believe this will free you (and others through you) from evil?

Friday: Mark 7:31-37. "Then looking up to heaven [Jesus]
sighed and said to him 'Ephphatha!' that is, 'Be opened.'
And immediately his ears were opened, his tongue was
released, and he spoke plainly." When these words were said
to you at your Baptism, what happened? Why does the
ability to hear God's word give you the ability to speak?

Saturday: Mark 8:1-10. Jesus said, "I have compassion for the crowd, because they have been with me now for three days and have nothing to eat." Does Jesus feel deeply our need for nourishment today? How does he respond? How do you?

Living This Week's Gospels

As Christian: Finish this one line: "I find meaning in life from...." Evaluate your answer.

As Disciple: Each day pick one situation that needs healing and find words of Jesus that apply to it.

As Prophet: Go to daily Mass this week as an expression of your belief that only union with Jesus gives meaning and healing power to your life.

As Priest: Bring someone who needs healing into deeper contact with the word of God (talk, write, invite, form a group).

As King: Ask what concrete, physical actions (at work, at home, in social life) show that you live no longer for yourself, but for God, to continue Christ's mission on earth. Find some visible way to keep you conscious of this when (and where) you tend to forget it.

Sixth Sunday of the Year

A Healing Community

Leviticus 13:1-2, 44-46; 1 Corinthians 10:31;
Mark 1:40-45 to 11:1

There is a thought-provoking contrast between the laws for dealing with leprosy in Leviticus and Mark's story of Jesus healing a leper. Before Jesus, the Jewish priests did not cure leprosy; they just declared officially that it was or was not present. Secondly, the "leper" had to live outside the camp, apart from the community, until healed (this was not the Hansen's disease we call leprosy, but a less serious skin disorder).

When the leper came to Jesus, he was cured. And then it was Jesus who had to stay out of town! He could not "enter a town openly. He remained outside in deserted places."

Before Jesus the community of the people of God had to protect itself by excluding the sick and the sinful. The full power to heal was not present, and so the infection of both sin and disease had to be kept out of the body of the community. Those who committed serious sins, such as murder, adultery, blasphemy, or even obdurate disobedience to parents, were to be expelled or killed: "Thus shall you purge the evil from your midst." But Jesus reversed this policy. When he purified the temple "the blind and the lame came to him in the temple, and he cured them." He described his Kingdom by telling of a king who sent servants out into the streets to gather all they found, bad and good alike. Jesus sends his disciples to bring all the infection in the world into his Church so that he might heal all. His presence makes the community strong enough, not only to fight off, but to heal all infection (see Deuteronomy 21:21; Matthew 21:14; 22:10).

The Church fights infection and heals by treating her members with "word and sacrament." The reason Jesus had to stay out in the desert after he healed people was that he did not want to be identified as a Messiah who healed physical afflictions by working miracles. He came for a greater healing: to overcome the woundedness of sin by sharing with us his own divine life (grace). His ministry was first to teach and proclaim the Good News. He also cured; but when he did and so many people flocked to him for healing that he could not teach or preach any more, he left that town, saying "Let us go on to neighboring towns, so that I may proclaim the message there also; for that is what I came out to do" (see Mark 1:38).

The power to heal exists still in Christ's Church; but that power works through the preaching and teaching of the Church, and through the sacraments. The power to heal physical sickness is ordinarily exercised through the Sacrament of Anointing (within which the word of God is also proclaimed). But the sure and certain effect of this sacrament is peace, comfort and strength to the soul: God always offers this through the sacrament, although he does not always give healing to the body.

The healing of sin, however, and of all the woundedness caused by sin—not just by our own, but by all the sinfulness of the world: the distorted attitudes and values, the false priorities programmed into us, the fears that hold us back from doing good, and the seductions which entice us to do evil—the power to heal us of this infection is always present and available in the Church. It is the power offered to us in "word and sacrament." If we want to be healed, we need large, repeated doses of God's word and God's sacraments: Mass, Communion, Reconciliation, and a conscious use of the gifts given to us through Baptism and Confirmation and through Matrimony or Holy Orders.

Any encounter with Jesus acting through his words, his sacraments, or through any member of his body, should be healing. But it is through and within the healing community of the Church, when we pray and study and respond to God's word together, that we experience the full healing power of Jesus.

Reflecting on This Week's Gospels

Sixth Week of the Year

> *Pray daily: Lord, wherever you are there is healing. Make me conscious that you are always present for me to answer my needs and in me to respond to the needs of others.*

Monday: Mark 8:11-13. "[Jesus] sighed deeply in his spirit and said, 'Why does this generation ask for a sign? Truly I tell you, no sign will be given to this generation.'" How can you, through love expressed, be a sign of Jesus' healing power?

Tuesday: Mark 8:14-21. Jesus said, "Watch out—beware of the yeast of the Pharisees..." The disciples concluded among themselves that Jesus said this because they had no bread. On a daily basis, are you more concerned about physical details or about your attitudes?

Wednesday: Mark 8:22-26. Jesus took the blind man by the hand and led him out of the village. Putting spittle on his eyes he laid his hands on him and asked, "Can you see anything?" Looking up he replied, "I can see people, but they look like trees, walking." Why does Jesus take us apart from the crowd at times to heal us? Why does he heal us only gradually? What are we required to do?

Thursday: Mark 8:27-33. "[H]e began to teach them that the Son of Man must undergo great suffering, and be rejected...and be killed, and after three days rise again.... And Peter took him aside and began to rebuke him." Why did Jesus choose to heal the word by suffering with love? How would you like him to heal it? Why is his way better?

Friday: Mark 8:34 to 9:1. "What will it profit them to gain the whole world and forfeit their life?" What are you most concerned about in life? What do you want relief or healing from? Is this the most important thing you should be concerned about?

Saturday: Mark 9:2-13. Then a cloud came, casting a shadow over them; then from the cloud came a voice, "This is my Son, the Beloved; listen to him!" What can you expect to receive if you "listen" to Jesus? How can you do this? How much time do you spend now listening to him?

Living This Week's Gospels

As Christian: Go to Jesus and ask to be "made clean." Specify from what.

As Disciple: Write out a "prescription" for yourself for Lent that will make your spiritual life more healthy.

As Prophet: Ask how you can make this Lent bear witness to you, give you a conviction that your faith, your hope, your love for God are real.

As Priest: Seek out a "leper"—someone everybody avoids or just forgets—and bring that person healing by some act of love.

As King: Identify some affleiction or woundedness that diminishes the joy, peace or spirit of love where you live, work or recreate. Ask some others you feel comfortable with if they "choose" to do something about it. First pray together.

Seventh Sunday of the Year

Sin, Anger and Love

Isaiah 43:18-19, 21-22, 24-25; 2 Corinthians 1:18-22;
Mark 2:1-12

For a few minutes, the paralytic to whom Jesus said, "Son, your sins are forgiven" had to be the most disappointed man in Israel. He was hoping to be healed of his paralysis. Instead, Jesus forgave his sins. If you had been he, which would you have preferred?

Jesus did heal his paralysis. But first he forgave his sins to show what was really more important. The man came asking for a cure; Jesus asked him first for a conversion. In effect Jesus was saying to him, "Your heart and soul are more paralyzed by sin than your body is by this disease." Jesus freed him from both.

We tend to think of sin as if it were just an offense against God and other people. But sin is before anything else an act of self-violation, an assault on our own being. Sin damages us. It does something to the orientation of our hearts. It alters our personalities, makes us different. Every free choice is an act of self-creation. Sin is an act of self-destruction. And every act of conversion and repentance rebuilds us.

When God is presented in Scripture as being "angered" by sin, what does this mean? We often think when people are angry at us that they do not love us. But no one can get as angry at us as those who love us most, because they are the ones who care the most about what we are doing to ourselves. That explains why no one can get as angry at us as God.

Saint Thomas Aquinas teaches that God created us with a capacity for anger for the sake of self-defense. This does not mean anger is to help us fight better. Anger often does lead to physical violence or verbal abuse, but that is a misuse of anger. The true, the good way to use anger is to let it energize us to protect ourselves or others against sin; to fight, not against other people, but against what threatens their well-being. Anger is not to help us hurt or destroy ourselves or others, but to help us protect and heal. Anger itself has no moral value; it is not a sin to be angry. Anger is good, because it is a natural reaction that is part of the being God gave us. But the way we use anger can be good or bad, life-giving or destructive, an act of love or of hate—for other people or for ourselves.

When Scripture presents God as being "angry" with sinners, this is a way of saying that God cares about what people do to themselves or to others. God does not want people hurt. He does not want our lives diminished, our beauty tarnished, our minds messed up or our wills enslaved or paralyzed. He wants us free, able to see and to do at every minute what is best for ourselves and for others.

A unique thing about God is that God does not take sides the way we do. When our love for family, friends or nation makes us angry at what other people are doing to them, we call the others "enemies" and we want to hurt or destroy them. God calls everyone his children, and when he is angry at what some people are doing to others, he wants to defend and save them both. God does not defend some of his children by destroying others. And he calls us to be like him in this. That is why Jesus taught, "Blessed are the peacemakers, for they will be called children of God.... Love your enemies and pray for those who persecute you, so that you may be children of your Father in heaven."

The problem is, we feel unable to do this, unable to love others as Jesus loves us. We cannot even convince ourselves always that what Jesus teaches is really true and right. Our minds and wills are paralyzed by fixations we got from our culture: fixations on power, success, reputation, retaliation, national and self-defense, survival. We cannot believe that the best defense is to lose our lives—or anything else that we would hurt others to defend—in order to find them. Like the paralytic, we need Jesus to say, "I free you from your sins" before we can rise and walk.

Reflecting on This Week's Gospels

Seventh Week of the Year

Pray daily: Lord, you came that we might have life and have it to the full. Free me from anything that holds me back from the fullness of response to you. I know that your words are life. Enable me to hear them and live.

Monday: Mark 9:14-29. "Teacher, I have brought you my son; he has a spirit that makes him unable to speak.... I asked your disciples to cast it out, but they could not do so." Do you believe that the priest has the authority in the sacrament of Reconciliation to free you from all of your sins? How much use do you make of this?

Tuesday: Mark 9:30-37. Then he sat down, called the Twelve, and said to them, "Whoever wants to be first must be last of all and servant of all." Do you judge yourself by this teaching of Jesus? What do you bring to the Sacrament of Reconciliation besides sins against the commandments God gave through Moses?

Wednesday: Mark 9:38-40. "Whoever is not against us is for us." Is this your attitude? Does your way of dealing with people reveal that you look upon them as brothers and sisters in Christ?

Thursday: Mark 9:41-50. "Salt is good, but if salt has lost its saltiness, how can you season it? Have salt in yourselves, and be at peace with one another." Is there anyone with whom you are not at peace? If so, what are you doing about it?

Friday: Mark 10:1-12. Jesus told them, "Because of your hardness of heart he wrote this commandment for you." Do you have reason to believe there is something God wants of you which he is not saying plainly because of the hardness of your heart? Is there anything you are unwilling to give him?

Saturday: Mark 10:13-16. "Truly I tell you, whoever does not receive the kingdom of God as a little child will never enter it." In what ways are you conscious of accepting the reign of God as a little child? Have you become stuck in an adult's acquired notions of the way things should be? Does this close you to any new life or directions adopted by the Church?

Living This Week's Gospels

As Christian: Think of any sin or fault that paralyzes you. Ask Jesus as Savior to free you from that sin and to let you rise and walk.

As Disciple: Read and reflect on the words of absolution used in the Sacrament of Reconciliation until you absorb their meaning (see the *Catechism of the Catholic Church,* #1449).

As Prophet: Think of any relationship between you and another which is "paralyzed" because of some unforgiven offense. Make some gesture to break the deadlock.

As Priest: Think of anyone you know who seems to be paralyzed by sin. The problem could be addiction, some hurt or misunderstanding that is keeping someone from Eucharist, or just discouragement. Reach out in any way you can.

As King: Ask what attitudes, values or priorities are "paralyzing"—that is, holding back from doing greater good—a group with which you work, live, recreate or pray. See if there is something you can do to address the problem and initiate a change.

Eighth Sunday of the Year

New Wine, New Hearts

Hosea 2:16-17, 21-22; 2 Corinthians 3:1-6; Mark 2:18-22

Jesus did not come to establish right order on earth. He came to establish right order within the minds and hearts of all who would believe in him. There is an enormous difference between these two ways of understanding Jesus as Savior.

The Messiah people expected—and wanted—Jesus to be was a Messiah who would clean up the environment: who would stop wars (by making war and winning), stamp out crime, eliminate poverty and make it possible for everyone to enjoy life on earth. And this, if we are honest with ourselves, just may be the kind of Savior we ourselves want him to be.

We all want to "get to heaven," of course (and isn't it interesting that the phrase suggests just a change of environment?)—but what is it we ask God for most often? Isn't it for things we think will make us able to enjoy life more on earth? We pray for health, for employment, for success, for better (less painful?) relationships with others. And we pray that our children will live good lives because we love them.

Why don't we pray more that we ourselves will live good lives? Is it because "good" for us means nothing more than lives free of the sins that hurt us and make us unhappy? Do we really want to live the kind of life Jesus teaches? Do we pray to enter into complete understanding of the Sermon on the Mount, and of everything Jesus taught? Do we pray for the grace to "be perfect as our heavenly Father is perfect"? Do we pray for the courage to "lose our lives in order to find them"? Do we pray to love others—all others—as Jesus loves us?

When people asked Jesus why his disciples did not fast,

he answered by teaching that what people do is not nearly so important as why they do it. Jesus sees little value in people fasting—or performing any other religious act—unless it is the true expression of their hearts, an act that expresses something they personally understand and desire. Jesus does not just want people at Mass, for example; he wants us to understand what is happening at Mass and desire to be part of it. He wants us to participate in the liturgy fully, actively and consciously.

That is why God will not use divine force to bring about justice and peace on earth. A world with no war, crime or even sin would not be pleasing to God unless the people in that world were really converted, really in agreement with God in mind and will and heart. If people did all the right things without personally embracing the values involved, the world would be a nicer place to live in, but the people would not be much better. What Jesus came to save was people, not just the circumstances they live in.

We would make a big mistake if we concluded from this that we should not keep any laws we do not understand or agree with. All good laws, especially the laws of God, are meant to teach us values. But some values we cannot understand or appreciate, especially when we are younger, unless we just keep the law out of obedience until experience shows us why. It is not keeping laws that is wrong, but keeping them without trying to appreciate them. It is good to go to Mass whether we understand it or not; but it is wrong to go to Mass without trying to understand what it is all about.

God loves us the way a bridegroom loves his bride. What he wants is our conversion to him in mind and will and desire. "I will lead you into the desert," he says, "where you can be alone with me, and I will speak to your heart. I will espouse you to me forever, and you shall know the Lord." Those who meet Jesus do not come away from that encounter "carrying, like Moses, tablets of stone in their hands; but carrying the Holy Spirit in their hearts, having become by his grace a living law, a living book, written not with ink but by the Spirit of the living God" *(The Splendor of Truth, #24).*

Reflecting on This Week's Gospels

Eighth Week of the Year

> *Pray daily: Lord, pour out the new wine of your Spirit into my soul. Lead me into the desert and speak to my heart. Write your law, your love, on my heart and espouse me to yourself forever.*

Monday: Mark 10:17-27. Jesus, looking at him, loved him and said to him, "Go, sell what you own, and give the money to the poor...then come, follow me." What radical gestures have you made to show the priority Jesus has in your life?

Tuesday: Mark 10:28-31. "[T]here is no one who has left house or [family] or fields for my sake and for the sake of the good news, who will not receive a hundredfold now in this age...." Do you believe this? What in your life shows it?

Wednesday: Mark 10:32-45. "[W]hoever wishes to become great among you must be your servant, and whoever wishes to be first among you must be the slave of all." Do you find your greatest sense of accomplishment in serving others? How do you do that?

Thursday: Mark 10:46-52. Jesus said to him in reply, "What do you want me to do for you?" The blind man replied to him, "My teacher, let me see again." What do you want Jesus to do for you? How do you show it?

Friday: Mark 11:11-26. "So I tell you, whatever you ask for in prayer, believe that you have received it, and it shall be yours." What kind of things can you believe absolutely God wants to give you?

Saturday: Mark 11:27-33. As he was walking in the temple area, the chief priests, the scribes, and the elders approached him and said to him, "By what authority are you doing these things?" How much authority do you give Jesus over your life? Why?

Living This Week's Gospels

As Christian: Begin to say a short prayer before everything you do—at home, at school, at work, with friends—to express (to yourself) your need for Jesus as Savior.

As Disciple: Read one passage of Scripture daily, asking if there is anyone with whom you could share your ideas on it.

As Prophet: Systematically go through common elements of your life-style—speech, dress, body language, use of time, money—asking what you are expressing about yourself and your belief in Jesus Christ.

As Priest: Try to speak in a "foreign tongue" this week by making an effort to communicate with someone you do not like very much or feel you do not understand.

As King: Make a list of five things you would like to change in your own world—family or social life, school or business — if you had the power. Then dream.

Ninth Sunday of the Year
The Sabbath Sign
Deuteronomy 5:12-15; 2 Corinthians 4:6-11; Mark 2:23 to 3:6

It seems strange to us today that the Pharisees would want to kill Jesus just because in their eyes he was working on the sabbath. Our society, though Christian in name, does not take seriously the commandment to set aside one day a week as a day of complete rest. Christians will work on Sundays (our sabbath since Jesus rose that day) or shop at stores that are open on Sundays almost without thinking about it.

For the Jews, however, observing the sabbath was a fundamental sign of belonging to the People of God. "Keep holy my sabbaths," God said, "as a sign between me and you to show that I am the Lord, your God."

To observe the sabbath did not mean to go to the temple; it meant to rest entirely from all work: "Six days you shall labor and do all your work. But the seventh day is the sabbath to the LORD your God; you shall not do any work...." It was taken so seriously that not to observe it was seen as denying the covenant and breaking away from the People of God. It was high treason and the law said, "[W]hoever does any work on the sabbath day shall be put to death."

Why was the sabbath taken so seriously? The sabbath observance expressed the fundamental relationship between God and human beings which God wanted to make crystal clear to the world by embodying it in his chosen people. "The Israelites shall keep the sabbath...as a perpetual covenant. It is a sign forever between me and the people of Israel."

What was the sabbath a sign of? God called it a sign "to show that it was I, the Lord, who made you holy." Resting one day a week is a sign—an expression and a learning experience—that human beings are "holy," or "sacred," which means "set apart." Humans are not like the rest of creation. Everything else in the world exists only for the sake of what it contributes to the well-being of the universe. Nothing has any reason for existing except to perform its function; that is, to "work." Nothing, that is, except humans.

Human beings do not exist just for the sake of what they do in the world. They exist for God. They have a direct, immediate relationship with God. In this, people are different from everything else that God created: everything else on earth was made for the human race, but the human race was made for God. And the way God teaches this is to require all human beings on one day a week to stop working so that they will know work is not the reason for their existence. One day a week they must let the world get along without them.

This teaches us the absolute sacredness of human life. Plants and animals may be killed and eaten, but not humans. Any other form of life which is a danger to the environment may be exterminated; but no human life may be destroyed for any reason at all. Humans do not exist for the sake of the environment, or even for what they can contribute to the human race, and therefore they cannot be destroyed when they are no longer useful, or even when they are a positive threat to the well-being of others. Humans exist for God directly, and no one but God can say when a human person who exists immediately for him may be destroyed.

Jesus brought to perfection what God had begun to teach through his law. The meaning of the sabbath, he taught, is that no one can be killed even for breaking the sabbath. "The sabbath was made for humankind, and not humankind for the sabbath." Christians will not kill even to preserve their own lives in this world, because we do not exist for this world but for eternal union with God. The life we preserve is the life Jesus gave us by rising from the dead. "We are always being given up to death for Jesus' sake, so that the life of Jesus may be made visible in our mortal flesh."

Reflecting on This Week's Gospels

Ninth Week of the Year

> *Pray daily: Lord, deepen in my heart the awareness that you have made me for yourself. Teach me to live for you, to long for you, to make everything in my life an expression of my love for you.*

Monday: Mark 12:1-12. "The stone that the builders rejected / has become the cornerstone; / this was the Lord's doing, / and it is amazing in our eyes." How do you make Jesus Christ the cornerstone of all your relationships with others?

Tuesday: Mark 12:13-17. Jesus said to them, "Give to Caesar what is Caesar's, to God what is God's." They were utterly amazed at him. Is there anything you have or do that is not God's? Has politics become in any sense or degree a religion for me?

Wednesday: Mark 12:18-27. "When they rise from the dead, they neither marry nor are given in marriage, but they are like angels in heaven." How much does your understanding of the relationship you will have with others in heaven influence your attitude toward them now?

Thursday: Mark 12:28-34. "You shall love the Lord your God with all your heart.... You shall love your neighbor as yourself." Can you cultivate love for God and treat people you do not know as mere strangers?

Friday: Mark 12:35-37. "David himself calls him [the Messiah] Lord; so how can he be his son?" If Jesus, though God, is a real member of the human family, what kind of real relationship do we, as members of his body, have with other people, even strangers?

Saturday: Mark 12:38-44. "For all of them have contributed out of their abundance; but she out of her poverty has put in everything she had, all she had to live on." How can you give "all you have" to God through what you do for others?

Living This Week's Gospels

As Christian: Set aside one day a week for a real "Sabbath" —a day of leisure—on which you do not do anything (barring emergencies) just because it has to get done.

As Disciple: Read Exodus 20:8-11 and Exodus 31:12-18.

As Prophet: Resolve not to do any shopping on Sunday as an expression of your belief that Sunday is not a day for business.

As Priest: Take part in the Sunday Eucharistic celebration as fully, actively and consciously as if you were the priest presiding at the liturgy. See what difference it makes in your devotion.

As King: Examine what keeps Sunday from being a day of complete rest for you—or for anyone who works for you. Think seriously about what you can do to change that.

LENT

Ash Wednesday and Weekdays After Ash Wednesday

Reflecting on This Week's Gospels

Pray daily: Lord, you call me out into the desert with yourself. You want to speak to my heart. Give me the motivation to break with the distractions in my life and focus my attention on your words. Amen.

Ash Wednesday: Matthew 6:1-6, 16-18. Jesus said, "Beware of practicing your piety before others in order to be seen by them; for then you have no reward from your Father in heaven." What personal, private acts of devotion tell you that religion is very personal to you and not just something you were "brought up in"?

Thursday after Ash Wednesday: Luke 9:22-25. "If any want to become my followers, let them deny themselves and take up their cross daily and follow me." How much of a cross is it to make time for daily Mass or prayer? How might this save you from greater crosses?

Friday after Ash Wednesday: Matthew 9:14-15. Jesus said, "The wedding guests cannot mourn as long as the bridegroom is with them, can they? The days will come when the bridegroom is taken away from them, and then they will fast." What does fasting express for you? What does it make you aware of?

Saturday after Ash Wednesday: Luke 5:27-32. Jesus said, "Those who are well have no need of a physician, but those who are sick; I have come to call not the righteous but sinners to repentance." What is healthy in your spiritual life? Where is growth needed? Have you experienced Jesus inviting you to more?

Several Suggestions for Lent

Prayer: Do something different. Add or change something in the way of you pray.

Fasting: Change something in your life-style: Make it simpler.

Almsgiving: Find a new way to give love, help or more acceptance to someone in your life.

First Sunday of Lent

Fulfillment, Reign, Reform

Genesis 9:8-15; 1 Peter 3:18-22; Mark 1:12-15

Before his public ministry, Jesus was led into the "desert," where God had led his people before him to be formed for forty years. The "desert," for all of us, is a period of formation which we must experience in order to pass from slavery ("Egypt") into the true freedom of the promised land (the Kingdom of God).

To be free from slavery to sin we must "come out," separate ourselves, from "Egypt"—that is, from the culture that enslaves us by conditioning us to think and act like everyone else. This is not just a counter-cultural stance that identifies us with some other particular group, some subculture, that conditions us in turn to think and act as that group does. The desert is separation—emancipation—from all the cultures of this world. To go to the "desert" is to let ourselves be formed by God himself.

God called the Jews into the desert to form them together as his chosen people. And Jesus calls us to come with him into the desert to be formed by him into a people, into a community of faith and differentness: his Church. To be a member of the Church is to accept that emancipation which consists in a certain radical "separation" from every human society, state and culture. Christians never see themselves primarily as citizens of any country. We are always in some sense "foreigners" within any nation, because we are citizens of heaven. Our homeland is not here. We always feel like exiles and aliens, no matter what country we live in or what culture we belong to. Our allegiance to every government, and our identification with every race, culture or ethnic group, is always secondary to our allegiance to God and our identification with the people, the children of God all over the earth (see Hebrews 11:13-16 and 13:13-14; 1 Peter 1:17 and 2:4-12; Philippians 3:20; Ephesians 2:11-22).

Christians give to Caesar what belongs to Caesar, and to God what belongs to God; that is, we contribute to the national interests of our country in every way which does not conflict with our undivided loyalty to God (see 1 Peter 2:11-17). But for us all, "national interests" are relatively unimportant, in the sense that they are radically secondary to our real interests as the People of God. How can we who have renounced all interest in money and property as such (see Matthew 6:25-32 and 19:21; Luke 6:20-31) have the same concern about the economy that the government has, except insofar as it is directed toward helping the poor? How can we who do not care about saving our own lives in this world (see Matthew 16:24-28) agree with the "kill or be killed" philosophy of the state?

We expect to question the attitudes, values and way of life taken for granted even in our own families. When Jesus said, "I came to bring sons into conflict with their fathers and daughters with their mothers"; and when he said, "Call no man 'father' on earth, because you have only one real Father, who is in heaven" (see Matthew 10:34-39, 23:9), he called us into that "desert" of emancipation from loyalty to our family's attitudes and values which frees us in every generation to look at the Gospel with open minds, and see in it "new things as well as old" (see Matthew 13:52). This is what keeps the Church prophetic and alive. Prophets come out of the desert, and it is their voices crying in the wilderness that keep the people moving toward the Kingdom of God (see Matthew 3:1-4; Mark 1:3; Luke 3:2).

Lent is a time when we consciously go into the desert—that is, when we deliberately, explicitly try to reexamine and call into question those basic attitudes, values and assumptions on which we base our lives and our behavior. In the measure that we experience conversion during this time, and reshape, reform our lives, we will come more fully under the reign of God and into the fulfillment he promises.

Reflecting on This Week's Gospels

First Week of Lent

> *Pray daily:* Lord, take me out into the desert with you this Lent. Give me the motivation to spend some time alone with you. Speak to my heart. Change my focus. Teach me to live life to the full in love.

Monday: Matthew 25:31-46. "Then the king will say to those at his right hand, 'Come, you that are blessed by my Father, inherit the kingdom prepared for you from the foundation of the world; for I was hungry and you gave me food, I was thirsty and you gave me something to drink, I was a stranger and you welcomed me....'" Is helping others your first priority in life? Is it the guiding principle behind our national policies? (Reflect on the death penalty, our immigration policies, our motives for war).

Tuesday: Matthew 6:7-15. "Pray then in this way: Our Father in heaven, hallowed be your name. Your kingdom come. Your will be done, on earth as it is in heaven." When you say the Our Father, are you consciously trying to make the order of priorities Jesus gives here your own?

Wednesday: Luke 11:29-32. "The queen of the South will rise at the judgment with the people of this generation and condemn them, because she came from the ends of the earth to listen to the wisdom of Solomon, and see, something greater than Solomon is here!" What is the difference between what Solomon valued and what Jesus teaches us to value? Have you studied the wisdom of both? Where will you find it?

Thursday: Matthew 7:7-12. "Ask, and it will be given you; search, and you will find; knock, and the door will be opened for you." What do you ask God for most frequently? What do you seek? What do you want him to open to you?

Friday: Matthew 5:20-26. "For I tell you, unless your righteousness exceeds that of the scribes and Pharisees, you will never enter the kingdom of heaven." How does your way of living go beyond the letter of God's commandments?

Saturday: Matthew 5:43-48. "For if you love those who love you, what reward do you have? Do not even the tax collectors do the same? And if you greet only your brothers and sisters, what more are you doing than others? Do not even the Gentiles do the same? Be perfect therefore, as your heavenly Father is perfect." Are you as concerned about doing favors for people who do not treat you well as you are about showing love for your friends? What was Jesus' attitude?

Living This Week's Gospels

As Christian: Write down your guiding goal in life. Is the fulfillment you seek the same as that proclaimed by Jesus?

As Disciple: Read chapter 5 of Matthew (the Sermon on the Mount). Compare what Jesus says here to your own value system.

As Prophet: Make a resolution to do something during Lent which expresses a different set of values or priorities than that of the culture. It could involve, for example, your use of time or money, the way you relate to people, the way you act at work, the way you recreate.

As Priest: Enter into the Lenten liturgy as fully as you can. Begin making plans now to attend all the services in Holy Week.

As King: Do something to make those choices in your life or home, or those policies at work over which you have some control express the priorities of God rather than of the culture. Look at how money is spent or made, how people are rewarded or punished, how truth is expressed or distorted.

Second Sunday of Lent

Religion Transfigured

Genesis 22:1-2, 9, 10-13, 15-18; Romans 8:31-34;
Mark 9:2-10

Before the Transfiguration, Jesus' disciples thought of him as "just" the Messiah. This made him great, of course, but not as great as Moses (through whom God gave the Law itself to Israel), or Elijah (the first of the great prophets). The Messiah was the "second David," the king who was supposed to "restore sovereignty" to Israel (see Acts 1:6). Compared to Moses and Elijah, who symbolized the Law and the Prophets, the Messiah was like the repairman compared to the architect.

The underlying assumption was that God had already set up the structure, doctrines and laws of his people, and there were no fundamental changes to make. The Messiah was just supposed to set Israel free to be the kind of people it already was, with the kind of religion it already had. Jesus' Transfiguration changed all that!

Peter thought he was paying Jesus a compliment by putting him on a par with Moses and Elijah by his suggestion of "three booths." God the Father is quick to dispel any notion that Jesus is just one of the "big three!" Jesus is not on the same level as Moses, Elijah or any other human hero. He is unique, exalted beyond imagination. He is God's "beloved Son." His transfigured appearance was a hint of his glory—and a clue to what he came to do.

Jesus did not come to do away with the Law and the Prophets (see Matthew 5:17-20), nor did he come just to restore them to full strength and perfect observance. He came to "fulfill" them—to bring them to a perfection as different from what people saw in them as the appearance of the transfigured Jesus was different from that of an ordinary human being. Jesus came to make his people divine as he was divine: to make the Law a law of divine behavior; to make the religion of Israel a religion of grace, of divine life; to transfigure the People of God as he was transfigured.

Jesus said, "Unless your holiness goes way beyond the law observance of the scribes and Pharisees, you can't say you are living under the rule of God" (see Matthew 5:20, my translation). How far beyond "keeping the rules" should Christian morality go? The answer is: "As far as the transfiguration of Jesus went beyond normal human appearance!" The behavior of Christians should stand out in the world the way a transfigured Jesus would stand out walking down Main Street (see Philippians 2:15-16; 2 Peter 1:19; 1 John 2:8).

The Transfiguration was a preview of the Resurrection. The risen Jesus lives today in us, in all who have surrendered themselves through Baptism to become his body on earth. And his glory shines out through us in the measure that our behavior reveals the presence of his Spirit in our flesh. When our human conduct—our decisions, choices, actions— can no longer be explained except as the expression of Christ's divine life in us, then Jesus is glorified in us (see John 16:13-14; 17:9-26; 2 Thessalonians 1:11-12).

This calls us to see ourselves, to understand our lives in this world, in a way that transforms our whole standard of morality. The goal and aim of our existence on earth, and of every action of our lives, should be to glorify Jesus by letting his light, his life, shine out in us. This is another way of saying that bearing witness to the Good News, witness to the mystery of Christ's death and Resurrection and presence to the world now in us, should be our first objective, concern and priority in every single moral decision and action of our lives.

In particular this must be the concern of the laity, because it belongs to the laity as their proper role and call in the Church, to carry the light of the Gospel into the "real world" of business and politics, of family and social life (see Vatican II, *Lay Apostolate,* #2 and #7). This is the crying need of our day.

Reflecting on This Week's Gospels

Second Week of Lent

Pray daily: Lord, give me the appreciation for you that your disciples had after seeing you transfigured. Teach me to live a transfigured life in imitation of you whose body you became through baptism.

Monday: Luke 6:36-38. "Be merciful, just as your Father is merciful." Do you consciously try to take the attitude toward everyone that God the Father takes? Do you look on everyone you deal with as family?

Tuesday: Matthew 23:1-12. "The scribes and the Pharisees sit on Moses' seat; therefore, do whatever they teach you; but do not do as they do, for they do not practice what they preach." Do you use the example of other people, even priests and bishops, as an excuse for not setting your ideals by the example and words of Jesus?

Wednesday: Matthew 20:17-28. "You know that the rulers of the Gentiles lord it over them, and their great ones are tyrants over them. It will not be so among you; but whoever wishes to be great among you must be your servant...." If you lived this consistently, how would it transform your life? If all Christians did, how would it transform the Church? How can you start with your own life?

Thursday: Luke 16:19-31. "If they do not listen to Moses and the prophets, neither will they be convinced even if someone rises from the dead." How has the Resurrection of Jesus transformed human life? Your life? Do you live in awareness of this?

Friday: Matthew 21:33-43, 45-46. "'The stone that the builders rejected / has become the cornerstone; / this was the Lord's doing / and it is amazing in our eyes.' Therefore, I tell you, the kingdom of God will be taken away from you and given to a people that produces the fruits of the kingdom."

What, precisely, do people reject in Jesus that you accept? What visible signs are there in your life that you accept this?

Saturday: Luke 15:1-3, 11-32. I shall get up and go to my father and I shall say to him, "Father, I have sinned against heaven and against you; I am no longer worthy to be called your son; treat me like one of your hired hands." If God treated you as a hired worker instead of as his child, what differences would you expect to see in your life?

Living This Week's Gospels

As Christian: Try to imagine Jesus transfigured before your eyes. If you saw him like this, what difference would it make in your life?

As Disciple: Ask how being the body of Christ should transfigure what you do with your hands, your feet, your eyes, your ears, your mouth.

As Prophet: Each day do something "transfigured" and different with each of the senses or members mentioned above. Do something worthy of your sacredness as the Body of Christ.

As Priest: See how many faces you can transform this week by getting them to smile.

As King: Imagine you were declared a canonized saint because of the way you lived your family life, your student or professional life, your social life. What differences can you imagine that would merit this? See how many you can make happen.

Third Sunday of Lent

The Anger of Jesus

Exodus 20:1-17; 1 Corinthians 1:22-25; John 2:13-25

When Jesus drove the hucksters and money-changers out of the temple, was this the same Jesus who extended the commandment "You shall not kill" to forbid even anger, insults and interior contempt for others (see Matthew 5:21-26)? Is the Jesus whom we see knocking over tables and driving out animals with a whip the same Jesus who said, "turn the other cheek" and "love your enemies" (Matthew 5:38-48)?

Actually, what Jesus gives us here is an example of how to live out his teaching on anger. As one of the "capital sins," anger is a source of much evil. But this means abiding, chronic and usually unacknowledged anger which distorts our attitudes and infects our behavior. This happens when we let our anger "grow" in us. In itself, however, anger is just a natural reaction that is part of the human nature God created. There is no fault at all in feeling angry, any more than in feeling hungry or cold or scared. Like every emotion, anger can be put to good uses or bad. In today's Gospel Jesus shows us how to use anger as an expression of love.

Love seeks union of mind and heart. Love works through communication. Expressing anger can say to another how strongly one feels about something—even about that person. What father who appreciates how beautiful his daughter is could hear her use ugly words and not get angry? Anger that is a revelation of one's own heart for the sake of evoking a beautiful response from another's heart is love. Anger which just tries to silence—or to kill—another is not. Anger can energize us, bring us to life and empower us to act. If the expression of our anger brings others to life in a good way, and aims at this, it is love. To act out of anger in a way that kills something in another which could have blossomed into life is bad.

Jesus' anger in the temple showed how much he cared about people, and it was directed to bringing about a change of heart in those to whom he expressed it. Jesus did not insult the merchants. By quoting Scripture to them he acknowledged their faith and the bond he had with them as fellow Jews (see Matthew 21:13; Mark 11:17). By saying they had turned God's house into a "den of thieves" he was not saying they were bad people, but reminding them of how good they were called to be. When a mother tells her son his room "looks like a pigpen" she is saying precisely that he is not a pig and should not live like one. By expressing the anger he felt, Jesus was trying to show people what they were doing and how bad it was, so that they would change.

Jesus did no violence, either to persons or property. He knocked over tables full of money—which would not break. He picked up some pieces of rope and used them to drive out animals. He told the dove sellers to take their birds outside, but he did not release the doves to fly away. The violent expression of his feelings was for the sake of communication; it was not violence directed against anyone.

Jesus tried by his gesture in the temple to bring his enemies to truth, as he taught in the Sermon on the Mount (see Matthew 5:24-25). It was not going to work, and when it didn't he did not fight but let them "destroy the temple" of his body on the cross (see John 2:18-22). Jesus did not use anger to destroy others, but in the hope of bringing others to life, even when he knew it would lead to his own death.

Jesus was not a man who stood meekly by and let evil go unchallenged. He did not use violence to overcome evil, but he did take forceful measures against it. What he used above all was the testimony of the truth, to which he gave force through the passionate expression of his own feelings. The gentleness and respectful love of enemies he teaches is not an excuse to stand by and do nothing about evil. It is a call to risk speaking the truth and even to accept dying ourselves in an effort to bring people together in unity, love and peace.

Reflecting on This Week's Gospels

Third Week of Lent

*Pray daily: Lord, teach me to put aside all anger
except that which comes from love. And teach me
to use anger to affirm others' value, never to
insult them.*

Monday: Luke 4:24-30. "There were also many lepers in
Israel in the time of the prophet Elisha, and none of them
was cleansed except Naaman the Syrian." Read Naaman's
story in 2 Kings, chapter 5. How did the slave girl help him?
Whom could you help in the same way?

Tuesday: Matthew 18:21-35. "The servant who had been
forgiven a huge debt found one of his fellow servants, who
owed him a very small amount. He started to choke the man,
demanding, 'Pay back what you owe.'" Are you more likely
to seek out and deal with people who owe you (or have
wronged you), or to notice and take care of those whom you
can help?

Wednesday: Matthew 5:17-19. "[W]hoever does [the least
of the commandments] and teaches them will be called great
in the kingdom of heaven." Is your focus as a Christian just
to keep God's law yourself—or to help others keep it? How
can you "teach" others?

Thursday: Luke 11:14-23. "[W]hoever does not gather
with me scatters." Is it the person of Jesus that you try to
bring people into contact with? Or do you just talk about
"religion" and "the Church"? What is (and is not) the
difference?

Friday: Mark: 12:28-34. "The second [commandment] is
this, 'You shall love your neighbor as yourself.'" If you left
the Church, how would you want others to "seek you out"?
Do you welcome others' efforts to involve you more in your
parish? Why?

Saturday: Luke 18:9-14. "The Pharisee prayed, 'O God, I thank you that I am not like other people: thieves, rogues, adulterers, or even like this tax collector.'" When you see others' faults, are you more likely to judge and condemn them or to try to help and heal them? Is your basic attitude that of a judge or a minister of Christ's healing love?

Living This Week's Gospels

As Christian: Each time you get angry, ask how you can respond to the situation in a way that shows you are aware that Jesus, not you, is the Savior of the world.

As Disciple: List the three things that make you angry most often. Opposite each, list the value that you are trying to defend with your anger. Ask if there is a better way to defend it.

As Prophet: Each time you get angry or show impatience, do something loving for someone immediately afterwards (not necessarily the same person who made you angry).

As Priest: Each day go out of your way to do something loving for someone who has made you angry recently or frequently does so.

As King: See if you can change or remove one thing that irritates people or makes them angry where you live or work.

Fourth Sunday of Lent

Light and Dark

Chronicles 36:14-17, 19-23; Ephesians 2:4-10; John 3:14-21

Jesus did not come to condemn the world. He came that the world might be saved. This refers, not only to people, but to all the values in the world. Jesus did not come to condemn anything human. He came to save every activity people engage in from destructiveness, distortion and mediocrity.

More than this, Jesus came to bring every human activity to fulfillment; to lift up everything people do to a divine plane. The new law of Jesus is a law, not just for good human behavior, but for living on the level of God.

The paradox is that, just as Jesus had to be lifted up on a cross in order to be glorified (see John 3:14; 8:28; 12:32), so we have to die to our merely human ways of thinking and acting in order to become divine. In the same way, when we come into the light of Christ, many things which before we accepted as good and natural we now condemn as darkness by comparison. It is not that Christians or Jesus are taking a "condemnatory attitude" toward things. We just say with Saint Paul, "Yet whatever gains I had, these I have come to regard as loss because of Christ" (see Philippians 3:7-8; see also Matthew 16:26, Mark 8:36). But to those who have not come into the light, Christians can appear to be negative when they preach a higher ideal. When we are lifted up with Christ we do not put down anything human; we just see everything from a different perspective in the light of our call to be divine.

In our day the Church protests against many things that the world in general accepts as natural or even good: pragmatic war, divorce, business for profit only, abortion, racial and sexual discrimination, foreign policy based only on national interest, sex without marriage, capital punishment, nuclear testing and stockpiling, the arms race, the option to stop providing adequate public care for the poor, the old, and the emotionally disturbed in favor of leaving them dependent on private charities. All of the above are facts in American society. Many of them are embodied in policy or law. Most of them have been explicitly condemned by the U.S. bishops, not without criticism from Catholics and non-Catholics alike.

To take one of the most common examples, how easily do people take for granted today that Church teaching takes a negative attitude toward sex? And yet, if we look at Church teaching, what is hard to accept is how much positive value the Church proclaims in sex. Does it give more or less value to sexual intercourse to see this as more than just a way of saying, "I love you"—to see it as a deep, personal expression of the total gift of oneself to another forever? Are Catholics refusing to accept their sexuality if they say that the surrender of the body in intercourse is inauthentic sex so long as it does not express actual commitment—not just an intended or possible commitment, but the real gift of oneself already made in marriage? Those who say that intercourse is acceptable provided two people love each other—with or without the total commitment of marriage—are giving a much less radical value to the act. They are devaluing the currency of human sexual expression.

To understand Church teaching, it is not enough to look at what she condemns. Like Jesus, the Church is not here to condemn human values, but to save them—and to lift them up to the level of the divine life given to us in grace. And therefore, the Church's restrictions on war can only be understood in the light of the sacredness she recognizes in every human person; her stance toward profit for profit's sake only makes sense in the light of what Jesus says about money, property and the real purpose of life. And ultimately we can only understand the Church's teaching on sex by seeing every act of intercourse as an expression of the Body of Christ. Those truly committed to human values will welcome Christ's transforming light.

Reflecting on This Week's Gospels

Fourth Week of Lent

Pray daily: Lord, draw me to you. Draw me to your light. Draw me by your light and your love, that I might learn from you and live life to the full.

Monday: John 4:43-54. Jesus said, "Unless you see signs and wonders, you will not believe." What is your faith in the Church based on? What is it not based on?

Tuesday: John 5:1-3, 5-16. "The sick man answered, 'Sir, I have no one to put me into the pool when the water is stirred up.'" How can you help someone (yourself, perhaps?) who has been on the fringe of church involvement for years take the plunge into full liturgical participation?

Wednesday: John 5:17-30. "Very truly, I tell you, the hour is coming, and is now here, when the dead will hear the voice of the Son of God, and those who hear will live." Do you believe that those who are dead wood in the parish can come alive? How can you show this belief by trying to make it happen?

Thursday: John 5:31-47. "I have a testimony greater than John's. The works that the Father has given me to complete, the very works that I am doing, testify on my behalf that the Father has sent me." What have you experienced Jesus doing which bears witness to his presence in the Church?

Friday: John 7:1-2, 10, 25-30. "Jesus cried out as he was teaching in the temple, 'You know me, and you know where I am from.'" Do you know the Church by experiencing her power to teach and sanctify you? Do you know where she comes from, where and when and by whom the Church was founded? What is so important about this?

Saturday: John 7:40-53. The Pharisees said, "Surely you have not been deceived too, have you? Has any one of the authorities or of the Pharisees believed in him? But this

crowd, which does not know the law—they are accursed."
How much does your faith, and your expression of faith,
depend on what others believe, what others express?

Living This Week's Gospels

As Christian: Bring some doubtful issue in your life to the
Sacrament of Reconciliation, asking Christ to illumine it
with his light.

As Disciple: Take some moral teaching of the Church
which you find difficult to accept or follow and just ask what
human values it tries to defend, and how it tries to raise those
values to a higher plane.

As Prophet: Resolve never to use words which do not show
enlightened respect for the sacredness of the human body or
of human sexuality.

As Priest: Notice how many times people or categories of
people are spoken of disrespectfully. Whenever you hear
this, balance the picture by expressing the truth that has
been omitted.

As King: Try to identify precisely the values or priorities
behind ways of acting that are taken for granted in your
home or social group; behind policies that no one challenges
where you work or in your school. Point out the truth.

Fifth Sunday of Lent

To Save Our Souls

Jeremiah 31:31-34; Hebrews 5:7-9; John 12:20-33

When Jesus says, "Those who love their life lose it," (John 12:25; Matthew 16:25-26) this is a deliberate play on words. The word he uses for "life" is psyche, which means "soul." It refers to whatever it is that goes out of us when we die and, while we are alive, makes us the unique persons we are. The psyche is the spiritual core in us, the "self" which gives human value to life and survives death. Jesus is saying that if we focus on saving our lives we will lose the meaning and value of life itself.

This applies to more than physical survival. We can save our business or job while losing the joy prosperity could give us. We can save our country by means which destroy whatever gave the "American way of life" its original meaning and value. We can save a marriage by compromises which kill its soul, or seek fulfillment in a way that ruins us as persons.

The lesson of the cross is that crucifixion can be the only way to joy, and accepting the death of something we desire can be the only way to attain it. The key to this is to understand the role of the psyche in our lives. What does it mean to "save" or "lose" our soul?

It is too simplistic to say, "To save our soul is to get to heaven." Heaven and hell are not places but conditions of being. Our joy or misery after death comes from what we are. "Heaven" means to enjoy God's own happiness by sharing in God's own life. Our psyche is "in heaven" when it knows and loves in perfect union with God. We are "in hell" when our soul has nothing but itself to know and love. That is why we have already lost or found our souls—our selves, our lives—on this earth in the measure that we have rejected or accepted union with God through faith, hope and love.

The essential task of life, then, is to save—to preserve from corruption, to bring to total fulfillment—our souls, that inner core of self in each of us which is the seat of our knowing and choosing. Nothing can replace this or substitute for it. As Jesus said, "What do you gain by winning everything in the world if you lose your psyche, your inner self, in the process?" (Matthew 16:26). And to show how radically he meant—and believed—this, Jesus refused to save himself from the cross, and he refuses to be the kind of Savior whose pledge is to save us from death, oppression, sickness or emotional pain. He sometimes does save us from these, but that is not what he came to do, and that is not what salvation really means.

Giving this the acid test by applying it to one of the most challenging areas of daily life, Jesus abolished divorce. By doing so he changed the goal of marriage from a partnership aimed at mutual help and happiness on earth as described in the last chapter of Proverbs, to a school of enduring love. A "successful" marriage is not one in which the spouses make life more enjoyable for each other, but one in which both are learning to love. Even a crucifying marriage is a successful one if both partners are learning how to love, because then they are saving their psyches, their inner selves, their souls. They are becoming like God.

What Jesus promises is the power to save our souls by loving back no matter what happens to us. This is what he did on the cross, and it is what he does for us as Savior. This is the only thing he absolutely promises to do for us as Savior: to give us the power to love one another in the same way that he showed his love for us on earth—by loving back no matter what we suffer. We can only do this, of course, by loving God above all things as revealed to us by the Holy Spirit in our hearts.

When Jesus abolished divorce, what he really did was proclaim that we now have the power through grace to do what God alone can do: to speak a word whose effect endures forever. We can speak words of irrevocable commitment, of unconditional love. To do this is to experience what it means to save our soul.

Reflecting on This Week's Gospels

Fifth Week of Lent

> *Pray daily: Lord, you came that we might have life and have it to the full. Teach me to live by all of your teachings with trust, even when I cannot see how they are enriching or enhancing my life.*

Monday: John 8:1-11. Early in the morning [Jesus] came again to the temple area. All the people came to him and he sat down and began to teach them. Do you feel called to teach those around you? How could you?

Tuesday: John 8:21-30. "When you have lifted up the Son of Man, then you will realize that I am he, and that I do nothing on my own, but I speak these things as the Father instructed me." How does the act of sacrificing yourself for others in love make your witness to Christ credible? Have you ever experienced this?

Wednesday: John 8:31-42. "I declare what I have seen in the Father's presence; as for you, you should do what you have heard from the Father." In what ways have you heard the Father's voice calling you to minister to others? How much time do you spend "in the Father's presence," thinking about his desires?

Thursday: John 8:51-59. "Very truly, I tell you, whoever keeps my word will never see death." Do you really believe that by losing yourself in love for others you will have a happier life? How can you do this?

Friday: John 10:31-42. "If I do [the Father's works], even though you do not believe me, believe the works, so that you may know and understand that the Father is in me and I am in the Father." Have you ever felt, in ministering to others, that you are truly united with Christ and a child of God? What have you experienced?

Saturday: John 11:45-57. "It is better for you to have one man die for the people than to have the whole nation destroyed." Jesus sacrificed himself for the good of the whole human race. In how many ways, large or small, could you sacrifice yourself for the common good of the different communities you are involved with?

Living This Week's Gospels

As Christian: Ask yourself these hard questions: What are you willing to die for? What are you willing to sin for? What are you living for?

As Disciple: Think back: How has sinning enhanced your life? How diminished it? Have you ever experienced sin as making you lose your own deepest, personal identity and self?

As Prophet: Wear or put something in your office or room which expresses the fact that Jesus gave a whole new focus to life by dying and rising.

As Priest: Forgive in your heart (by wishing them conversion and life everlasting; not by trying to "feel good" about them) all who have injured you. If possible, do something loving for one of them, for example, by participating in Eucharist one weekday or saying some prayers for that person.

As King: Question in conversation how important "survival" is—for yourself, for the nation, for your school or business. See if survival seems to take precedence over serving God.

Sixth Sunday of Lent: Passion (Palm) Sunday

Hosannas and Holocausts

Isaiah 50:4-7; Philippians 2:6-11; Mark 11:1-10
(procession Gospel)

"Palm Sunday" is now called "Passion Sunday" to focus our attention on the meaning behind it all. Jesus entered Jerusalem with hosannas in the air and palms beneath his feet, the way victors entered conquered cities. In the eyes of the people, Jesus was restoring Israel's pride. He was saying to the world that God does what he promises to do, and he has the power to do it.

Jesus was in fact saying this about himself when he allowed the crowds to acclaim him as Messiah: Yes, he had come to fulfill God's promise. And, yes, he had the power to establish a new order that would renew the world. But that is where the similarity ends between his victory parade and every other.

By his victory parade Jesus gave a new meaning to victory, as he did to everything else. He entered Jerusalem to be handed over to his enemies. He would win by accepting defeat at their hands. For Christians, real victory is a triumph, not over other human beings, but over evil; not over evil people, but over the evil to which they, like ourselves, are enslaved. To triumph over an enemy without overcoming the evil which brought us into conflict in the first place is not victory but defeat.

That is why wars are never victories. Wars deal with the effects of sin while strengthening their causes. The U.S. bishops wrote: "The causes of war are multiple and not easily identified. Christians will find in any violent situation the consequences of sin: not only sinful patterns of domination, oppression or aggression, but the conflict of values and interests which illustrate the limitations of a sinful world." Every time we kill to protect our national interests we increase our attachment—and our enslavement—to those national interests. And they are usually the same national interests—prosperity, prestige and the balance of power to protect them—which motivated our enemy to go to war against us. Every war is a defeat, because every war adds to all sides' motivation for the next one.

The only real victory over evil is conversion, and wars never aim at that. But the conversion of the human race was the whole aim of Christ's passion. That was the victory he won. And the reason he won it was that he used, not violence and power, but love and surrender. He showed us that the only way to triumph over evil is to refuse to fight for the same values which give evil a hold on us or to use the same means which evil incites our enemy to use.

Jesus entered Jerusalem riding on a donkey to make it clear he was fulfilling the prophecy of Zechariah (9:9-10): "Shout aloud, O daughter of Jerusalem! / Lo, your king comes to you; / triumphant and victorious is he, / humble and riding on a donkey / ...He will cut off the chariots [the ancient equivalent of a tank] / ...and the war horse / ...the battle bow shall be cut off,/ and he shall command peace to the nations."

The victory of Jesus was a victory over idolatry. He could have defeated his enemies by inciting his followers to anger and violence, but that would have obscured, not revealed, his knowledge of the heart of God. Jesus came "to bear witness to the truth" (John 18:37). And the truth is that God is love, and all who worship the one true God must express their worship through acts of love. The victory of Jesus was in his refusal to win by means which would deny that God is the God he is.

Let us pray that war will never be a true revelation to the world of what America stands for. If in war we offer a hundred thousand victims on the altar of air power we pay implicit homage to Mars, god of war. And if, when death and destruction give us our victory, we celebrate in a liturgy of triumph, we are celebrating a tragedy that never should have happened. The liturgy of Passion Sunday gives us a contrast to reflect on.

Reflecting on This Week's Gospels

Sixth Week of Lent: Holy Week

Pray daily: Lord, teach me that the only effective power is the power of meekness and gentleness of heart. You came to save the world through love, not force. Give me the courage to let go of anything I cannot keep without giving up love.

Monday: John 12:1-11. "Mary took a pound of costly perfume made of pure nard, anointed Jesus' feet.... The house was filled with the fragrance of the perfume." What words or gestures of yours fill the church with your faith and love during liturgies.

Tuesday: John 13:21-33, 36-38. Jesus answered, "Will you lay down your life for me? Very truly, I tell you, before the cock crows, you will have denied me three times." How can you "deny Christ" by being afraid to live out your deepest values?

Wednesday: Matthew 26:14-25. Jesus said, "I will keep the Passover at your house with my disciples." What do you feel Jesus is asking of you? How can you prepare your house— where you live or work—for him?

Holy Thursday: John 13:1-5. "Now before the festival of the Passover, Jesus knew that his hour had come to depart from this world and go to the Father. Having loved his own who were in the world, he loved them to the end." Does the spirit of self-sacrificing love, shown in service for the sake of bringing people together in love, characterize everything you do?

Good Friday: John 18:1-19:42. "Pilate also had an inscription written and put on the cross. It read, 'Jesus of Nazareth, the King of the Jews.' Many of the Jews read this inscription, because the place where Jesus was crucified was near the city; and it was written in Hebrew, in Latin, and in Greek." Why did many Jewish leaders reject Jesus? The Romans? The Greeks? Do you accept him for these same reasons?

Easter Vigil (Holy Saturday has no Mass): Mark 16:1-8. "And very early on the first day of the week, when the sun had risen, they went to the tomb. They had been saying to one another, 'Who will roll back the stone for us from the entrance to the tomb?'" When Jesus seems absent from your life, how do you look for him? What obstacles to intimate union with him are you willing to roll out of the way?

Living This Week's Gospels

As Christian: Put a palm from the Passion Sunday liturgy in a place where you will see it all day, all year. Use it to remind yourself that the reign of Christ has begun; the achievement of goals through force and power has been discredited.

As Disciple: For each way that you see goals being achieved through force or intimidation, try to figure out a way to achieve them through persuasion and conversion of attitudes and values.

As Prophet: Each time you begin to get angry or to go on a power trip this week, repeat to yourself, "[L]earn from me; for I am gentle and humble in heart, and you will find rest for your souls."

As Priest: Ask what your predominant image is at work and at home: Is it more of power or of priesthood (that is, of sacrificial love in service to others for the sake of building community)? Which do you want?

As King: Ask how many things where you work or live are there just to express status or prestige. How many can you get rid of or change to express an accepting, family spirit of equal respect for all?

EASTER TRIDUUM

and EASTER

Easter Triduum
(Holy Thursday, Good Friday, Easter Vigil)

A Three-Day Sunday

Mass of the Lord's Supper (Holy Thursday)
Exodus 12:1-8, 11-14; 1 Corinthians 11:23-26;
John 13:1-15

Good Friday
Isaiah 52:13—53:12; Hebrews 4:14-16, 5:7-9;
John 18:1—19:42

Easter Vigil
At least three of seven Old Testament readings with
Psalm responses, always including the Exodus account:

Genesis 1:1—2:2; Genesis 22:1-18; Exodus 14:15—15:1;
Isaiah 54:5-14; Isaiah 55:1-11; Baruch 3:9-15,32—4:4;
Ezekiel 36:16-17a,18-28; Romans 6:3-11; Matthew 28:1-10

M any people think that we celebrate the Resurrection on Easter Sunday. To them, Good Friday is a tough day for remembering the crucifixion and Holy Thursday a sort of nice day when we think about the Eucharist and visit church. But Easter is Sunday.

At some point they may have been told that Easter is the greatest feast of the year, greater than Christmas. But that doesn't seem true: Nobody gets into Easter as much as into Christmas. And besides, at Christmas school is out for a week or more; Easter doesn't rate that.

Easter is really a three-day Sunday: a celebration of the resurrection that lasts from Holy Thursday evening to Easter Sunday evening.

Good Friday is all about resurrection, not crucifixion! Holy Thursday is a celebration of resurrection, too. The three last days of Holy Week are one long celebration of the Resurrection—and of Baptism.

The Easter liturgy (all three days) developed as the one great celebration of the year. It was the time when new Christians were baptized—and their Baptism was an initiation into the mystery of our redemption; that is, of our rebirth as children of God. The mystery is that we are saved and reborn only by dying and rising, by being baptized into the death and resurrection of Jesus. And this mystery is so central to our whole understanding of the Good News of Jesus that the Church spends three days every year celebrating it; presenting it to our senses; reading the Scripture texts that explain it; walking us through it; helping us feel it, appreciate it, experience it.

These three days bring home to us the meaning behind the words that invite us to celebrate on Sunday: "May the grace of our Lord Jesus Christ, and the love of God, and the fellowship of the Holy Spirit be with you all." They are the most important days of the year.

If Holy Thursday, Good Friday and Holy Saturday are part of the Easter Sunday celebration, why aren't we obliged to attend services those days? The answer is that ours is a religion of meaning, not of laws. Rules are necessary, of course, in any human community. But the early Christians would no more have thought of making a rule about attending Mass than they would have thought about making it a rule that parents should attend the weddings of their children! Some things are just obvious. The three days of Easter are the most important celebration of the liturgical year.

If we really understand Baptism, and what it means for us to be the Church, what it is to be the living Body of Christ on earth, we understand that the "liturgical year" is just everybody's year, everybody's life—with its meaning made explicit. We don't have any "real" life or "ordinary" life apart from our life as Church, our life as the Body of Christ. We have died, and our lives are hidden now in Christ. We live now, not just human lives, but Christ is living in us (see Colossians 3:3). To celebrate Easter, then, is to celebrate the meaning of life itself, of our lives. Given the relationship we have with Jesus Christ, it would make more sense for us to stay home from a daughter's wedding than from the Easter liturgy. If we felt our graced bond with Christ our Head as strongly as we feel the natural bonds of kinship, this would be obvious to us.

A meaningless life is hardly worth living. And meaning unrecognized cannot give direction to our love. During the Easter liturgy we celebrate the meaning and direction of life itself. That is why we give it three days.

Easter Sunday

Priests Minister

Acts 10:34, 37-43; Colossians 3:1-4 (or 1 Corinthians 5:6-8);
Mark 16:1-8 (or John 20:1-9)

Every baptized person is a priest. We were anointed with chrism and consecrated to fulfill the mission of Jesus as priest, prophet and king.

The angel at Jesus' empty tomb told the women, "He has been raised; he is not here!" Paul echoes these words to us, "...You were raised with Christ!" The angel continued, "[H]e is going ahead of you to Galilee; there you will see him." And Paul concludes, "Set your minds on things that are above, where Christ is!"

Both these texts speak of a *fact* and an *act:* the fact that Jesus has risen and that we have risen with him to new life; and the act of seeking him where he is. And the truth is, all our acts, and everything we seek in life, depend on how we understand the fact of our existence: what we are, what we are called and able to do that will give us meaning and fulfillment in life.

The basic fact of our baptized existence is simply "You have died, and your life is hidden with Christ in God." That is a fact, and that fact changes everything. Because we "set our minds on what is above, where Christ is," our whole outlook on life is different: we now think of what is above, not of what is on earth. Our life's goal and all our objectives, short-term and long-term, are on a different plane.

Concretely, what specific goal should give unity and direction to all our efforts? John Paul II teaches that "Jesus' way of acting and his words are the moral standard of Christian life"; that is, of Christian direction-setting. And he specifies: "Jesus asks us to follow him and to imitate him along the path of love which gives itself completely to the community out of love for God." *(The Splendor of Truth,* #20).

This amounts to priesthood: the priestly ministry to which every Christian is consecrated at Baptism. And the model for this "path of love" was presented by an earlier Pope in one of the earliest evangelizing sermons on record: "You know...how God anointed Jesus of Nazareth with the Holy Spirit and with power; how he went about doing good and healing all who were oppressed by the devil, for God was with him. We are witnesses..." (Acts 10:38).

That, in a nutshell, is what Jesus came out of the womb to do—and out of the tomb to continue doing. As he was anointed with the Holy Spirit and power during his earthly life, so is he still anointed in the risen life he lives in his Body, the Church. To all the baptized he says the words he first spoke to the apostles, "You will receive power when the Holy Spirit has come upon you, and you will be my witnesses."

The power we receive through the Holy Spirit is the power Jesus showed when he went about doing good and healing all those oppressed by the devil. We are empowered by the love of God poured out in our hearts to go about doing good—in family and social life, in business and politics—and to heal all those oppressed by the devil, who works through the darkness and distortions of our culture, or through the divisions and indifference to others which turn our communities cold.

All the baptized can echo Peter's words: "He commanded us to preach to the people...testify about him that everyone who believes in him receives forgiveness of sins through his name." Priests in Holy Orders are commissioned to minister publicly; that is, in the name of the whole community. Therefore they are bound by special ties of obedience to the bishop who, since he is responsible or "answerable" for anything done in the community's name, must have authority to regulate it. (Every right exists only by virtue of an obligation.) And when non-ordained priests do ministry that is public, this is always under the authority of the bishop, either directly or through a pastor. But the private exercise of priesthood in family, social life and business should be just as all-embracing and continuous as the ministry of the ordained. It was to continue serving as priest, both publicly and privately, that Jesus came out of the tomb. In all we do as his Body, whose life is hidden with Christ, our goal is to be his priests.

Reflecting on This Week's Gospels

First Week of Easter

Pray daily: Lord Jesus, you rose from the dead to continue your ministry as priest in me and in all who have become your Body by Baptism. Make me a faithful minister and witness to you. Help me to "go about doing good and healing" all I meet today.

Monday: Matthew 28:8-15. Then Jesus said to them, "Do not be afraid; go and tell my brothers to go to Galilee; there they will see me." Where, when, how do you "see" Jesus acting in your life? Is it when you try to minister to others?

Tuesday: John 20:11-18. Mary Magdalene went and announced to the disciples, that she had seen the Lord, and repeated what he told her. How have you experienced the risen Jesus? With whom have you shared this?

Wednesday: Luke 24:13-35. Then the two recounted what had taken place on the way and how he was made known to them in the breaking of the bread. How is the Mass an experience of the risen Jesus? Is it for you?

Thursday: Luke 24:35-48. "You are witnesses of these things." Do you think of yourself as a "witness" to the events of Christ's life? When, where, to whom should you be?

Friday: John 21:1-14. "He said to them, 'Cast the net to the right side of the boat, and you will find some [fish].' So they cast it, and now they were not able to haul it in because there were so many fish." When have you experienced Jesus filling your net? How often do you cast it?

Saturday: Mark 16:9-15. He said to them, "Go into all the world and proclaim the good news to the whole creation." Do you understand this as a mission entrusted to you? How are you fulfilling it?

Living This Week's Gospels

As Christian: Begin each morning this week by saying, "He is risen; he is going ahead of me." Then renew your baptismal commitment to live and work as his Body that day.

As Disciple: Each time a situation arises which calls for a response, ask how Jesus would handle it (or, if you only get time to reflect afterwards).

As Prophet: Each morning identify one thing you will be doing that day which in fact, recognized by others or not, bears witness to the risen Jesus living in you. Be conscious of that act or fact during the day.

As Priest: Each morning ask how you can "go about doing good and healing" that day. Be sympathetic to those who offend you.

As King: Ask what good initiatives you have been afraid to take—in family, social or professional life—and reflect on your fears in the light of Christ's victory over sin and death.

Priests Forgive Sins

Acts 2:32-35; 1 John 5:1-6; John 20:19-31

P riests ordained for public ministry forgive sins. So do priests consecrated by Baptism for private ministry— but in a different way.

All priests, that is, all the baptized, have the "ministry of reconciliation" Saint Paul speaks of (2 Corinthians 5:18). The ministry of reconciling people to God belongs to all Christians, just because we share in the priestly mission of Jesus. We should all proclaim reconciliation by encouraging people who are discouraged by their sins to believe in the love of God and seek relationship with him. We should also embody reconciliation by personally forgiving all who injure, betray or deceive us. Every Christian is an "ambassador for Christ" and a continuation of his healing presence in the world.

Ordained priests have a ministry of public reconciliation. To sin is to distance oneself in some way from God and the other members of the Church by words or actions incompatible with that divine life which the baptized, as the risen Body of Jesus, are committed to live. Every sin is in some way a denial of our communal commitment to live by faith in Jesus' teachings, by the new hope Jesus made possible and by the love he modeled for us. To reprofess one's commitment publicly through the Sacrament of Reconciliation is an act of "return and concern"—of return if we have broken our commitment by an act so incompatible with Jesus' teaching that it constitutes a "conversion away from" the goal of living divine life; of concern if our actions have just called into question how serious we are about it. In the Sacrament of Reconciliation the priest publicly and officially receives us back into full and acknowledged union with God and with the community in the name of the bishop who, as head of the local Church, can speak for all of its members and so for the Church and for Christ.

On the private level, however, we share in the Church's ministry of "reconciling penitents" every time we show our faith in the reality of another's commitment to Christ, our trust in another's ability to change; or extend to another person the healing love which Jesus extended to us all. One of the things which enables people to ask forgiveness through the Sacrament of Reconciliation is the love they experience from those members of the Body of Christ with whom they deal in daily life. The priestly ministry of the non-ordained makes the ministry of ordained priests credible.

The presence of an ordained priest makes it possible for the body and blood of Jesus to be made present and lifted up to the Father during Mass in continued reparation for the sins of the world. We often say the priest "offers Mass" (or "celebrates" or "says" Mass), as if this were something the priest alone did—or did alone. It is true that the ordained priest alone can do what the ordained priest does; but it is not true that he can, legitimately, at least, do it alone. The priest is ordained to preside—publicly and officially—at the Mass which the whole congregation is celebrating and offering. The ordained priest "offers" or "celebrates" only as one priestly member of a priestly congregation. Like the other priestly members, he has his own special role in the ceremony, just as every non-ordained priest in the congregation has.

At Mass all who were anointed at Baptism to share, as members of his body, in Jesus' mission as priest, prophet and king are lifting up the body and blood of Christ as "priests in the Priest," begging mercy for the world from "God, the Father of mercies, who through the death and resurrection of his Son has reconciled the world to himself and sent the Holy Spirit among us for the forgiveness of sins." Behind every Mass is the echo of Christ's words to the apostles: "Peace be with you. As the Father has sent me, so I send you.... Receive the Holy Spirit. If you forgive the sins of any, they are forgiven them."

Reflecting on This Week's Gospels

Second Week of Easter

> *Pray daily: Lord Jesus, at my Baptism you gave me the gift of the Holy Spirit and consecrated me as your priest. Teach me to offer myself and all around me at every moment for the life of the world.*

Monday: John 3:1-8. "Rabbi, we know that you are a teacher who has come from God, for no one can do these signs that you do apart from the presence of God." How does the love you show to others make it obvious that God is with you, in your heart?

Tuesday: John 3:7-15. "Just as Moses lifted up the serpent in the wilderness, so must the Son of Man be lifted up, that whoever believes in him may have eternal life." Are you conscious at Mass that you are "lifting up" the body and blood of Christ—and yourself in Christ—for the forgiveness of sins?

Wednesday: John 3:16-21. "God did not send the Son into the world to condemn the world, but in order that the world might be saved through him." When you see sin, do you respond as priest (with compassion, healing) or as judge (with condemnation, anger)? Is your response the same for all sins?

Thursday: John 3:31-36. "The one who comes from above is above all; the one who is of the earth belongs to the earth and speaks about earthly things." Does your conversation show that you are conscious of your priesthood—of being sent to witness, help and heal—in everything you do?

Friday: John 6:1-15. A large crowd followed Jesus because they saw the signs he was performing on the sick. Do people follow you—follow your example, follow you to church and religious functions—because they see the healing love you show to all around you?

Saturday: John 6:16-21. Jesus said to them, "It is I; do not be afraid." Do people feel safe around me? Confident that they will be respected, that their ideals will not be violated, that where you are the tone of conversation and behavior will be life-giving?

Living This Week's Gospels

As Christian: Every time you see something undesirable this week, ask what interaction with Christ could change that.

As Disciple: Read through the Eucharistic Prayer(s) of the Mass, noticing how "we" and "us" are used.

As Prophet: Each day look for one concrete thing you can do which will express belief in Christ's power to heal— everybody.

As Priest: Look for any signs of sadness in each person you meet. Ask the Holy Spirit what you can do that will be healing.

As King: With a sense of responsibility for the world, lift up to God in prayer, on the spot, anything you see or experience each day that is not as it should be in your environment.

Third Sunday of Easter

Priests Make Jesus Present

Acts 3:13-15, 17-19; 1 John 2:1-5; Luke 24:35-48

How do we know Jesus? What makes him real to us? Do we know him just as a memory, a historical event, a person who lived on earth two thousand years ago? Is it enough to read about him in Scripture and figure out through his words and actions what kind of person he was? Or is there a real, living contact with him now? Is Jesus risen from the dead to be with us here, on this earth, so that we might experience his presence now?

The Gospel tells us that it is in the Eucharistic celebration that we most clearly experience the real presence of Jesus. He was made known to the disciples "in the breaking of the bread." When Luke describes this encounter, he uses the formula all Christians were familiar with from the Mass: "[H]e took bread, blessed and broke it, and gave it to them...." We spontaneously want to continue: "saying, 'This is my body...'" (see also Matthew 14:19; 15:36).

In the Mass Jesus is present in three ways, and all three are important if he is to be made known to us in the breaking of the bread. First, he is present in the words of Scripture as they are read in the liturgy. Vatican II teaches, "The Church has always venerated the divine Scriptures just as she venerates the body of the Lord, since, especially in the sacred liturgy, she unceasingly receives and offers to the faithful the bread of life from the table both of God's word and of Christ's body.... [The Scriptures] make the voice of the Holy Spirit resound in the words of the prophets and Apostles.... In the sacred books the Father who is in heaven meets his children with great love and speaks with them" *(Dogmatic Constitution on Divine Revelation, #21)*. The reading of God's word, then, whether at home or in church, is a priestly act: It mediates the presence of God to all who hear. Reading Scripture privately prepares us for the public proclamation in liturgy.

When he appeared to his disciples, Jesus did more than open their minds to understand the Scriptures. He also said, "Touch me and see!" (See John 20:27.) In the Mass he gives us his Body and Blood. He comes to us in the breaking of the bread in a way that is tangible and physical. There is an experience of his presence—and of his love—in Holy Communion which is different from all others. Anyone who receives with conscious faith and attention can testify to this.

An ordained priest is required for the public liturgy which gives us the Body and Blood of Christ. But every priest present (all who are priests by Baptism) offers the sacrifice with him. And through the priesthood of the Eucharistic ministers who carry Eucharist to the sick and homebound, the blessing of Communion can be extended to all who desire it.

The presence of Jesus is also experienced in the community through the manifestation of the Spirit whose voice also resounds in each person's "full, conscious, active participation"—both internal and external—in what is being expressed. By words and body language, by responding to the prayers, by singing and moving in the gestures of the Mass, all who participate in the liturgy reveal the real presence of Jesus in the community.

At Mass we are in the real presence of Jesus offering himself on the cross. The Mass does not repeat the sacrifice of Calvary, but makes it truly present in our time and place. As his Body on earth now, baptized to be "priests in the Priest," we all perform with him in liturgy the priestly ministry of offering his body to the Father for the life of the world. And as "victims in the Victim," we all offer ourselves with him. The ordained priest speaks the words of offering publicly in the name of all, but all speak personally as priests through the words of the presider. We offer our bodies as a living sacrifice, committing ourselves to mediate the life of Christ to others by giving expression to his light and love in our bodies. This is priesthood.

Reflecting on This Week's Gospels

Third Week of Easter

Pray daily: Lord Jesus, I believe you are sharing with me your life and your priesthood. Teach me to "offer myself as a living sacrifice" with you at Mass and at every moment of my day.

Monday: John 6:22-29. "This is the work of God, that you believe in the one he sent." *Liturgy* means "work of the people." Do you work at full, conscious, active expression of faith during Mass?

Tuesday: John 6:30-35. So they said to him, "What sign are you going to give us then, so that we may see it and believe in you? What work are you performing? Our ancestors ate the manna in the wilderness; as it is written, 'He gave them bread from heaven to eat.'" What, for you, is the Eucharist a sign of?

Wednesday: John 6:35-40. "This is indeed the will of my Father, that all who see the Son and believe in him may have eternal life." How do you "see"—and help others to see—Jesus in the Eucharistic celebration?

Thursday: John 6:44-51. "The bread that I will give for the life of the world is my flesh." In how many ways does Jesus "give his flesh" to people today?

Friday: John 6:52-59. "Those who eat my flesh and drink my blood abide in me, and I in them." What does it mean to "abide" in Christ? How can you keep yourself constantly aware that he is abiding in you?

Saturday: John 6:60-69. Simon Peter answered him, "Lord, to whom can we go?..." Do you believe that Jesus gives you his own Body and Blood in Communion? How often do you go to him to receive him? To whom or what else do you go?

Living This Week's Gospels

As Christian: Seriously consider how often you can offer Christ and yourself at Mass during the week and receive the "bread of life."

As Disciple: Read the readings for next Sunday during the week to relish them more during the Mass (Acts 4:8-12; 1 John 3:1-2; John 10:11-12).

As Prophet: Decide on one action you can do this week which will be a sign of Christ's living presence in you because it cannot be explained any other way.

As Priest: Consciously offer the Body and Blood of Christ at Mass together with the presider, and offer yourself with him.

As King: Offer the Body and Blood of Christ in the Mass to bring about the changes in society needed to heal specific evils you are aware of—violence, crime, poverty, injustice, mental illness or situations you see at work or in your family or social life.

Fourth Sunday of Easter

Priests Shepherd the Flock

Acts 4:8-12, 17-19; 1 John 3:1-2; John 10:11-18

To be a shepherd means to take care of a flock, and to be a priest means to be dedicated to the service of a community. The sacrament of Baptism consecrates us to minister individually as priests in the name of Jesus Christ. The sacrament of Holy Orders consecrates us to minister in an official, public capacity in the name of the bishop or Church as well.

By the very fact of being priests, whether by Baptism or Holy Orders, we are already related to other people—to the Christian community and to all the "other sheep that do not belong to this fold"—in roles of service. We are personally committed and sacramentally consecrated to "the work of ministry, for building up the body of Christ" (Ephesians 4:12).

Priests do not "volunteer" for ministry. They are already committed to minister, and they simply choose or accept the particular ministries which the needs of the community, or their own gifts and circumstances, indicate that they should perform. This is true of all priests, of those ordained to publicly represent the Church, as the clergy are by Holy Orders, and of those consecrated to minister as individuals in the name of Jesus Christ, as the laity are by Baptism. Since all Christians are already committed as priests to "build up the body of Christ in love," the ministries they perform as members of their parish or diocese are not volunteer work but simply the particular functions for which they are individually designated as members of a working team.

Volunteers are people who offer to help others do something which is not their own responsibility and to which they themselves are not already committed. We volunteer to help our neighbors paint their house; but when it comes to painting our own house, all those who live there just pitch in and help. This is not volunteering; it is doing our part. The whole responsibility is shared by all, and each has a part, a particular role to play, in fulfilling it. This is the way it is in the ministry of building up the body of Christ to which all of us who are baptized are committed as priests of Jesus Christ. There is no question about whether we are committed to help; the only question is what form our contribution should take.

In the past we assumed, without thinking about it very explicitly, that the laity's role was just to "pay, pray and obey" while the clergy shepherded the flock. And it is true that a "pastor" is, in the words by which the Church defines herself, "the proper [official] shepherd of the parish entrusted to him, exercising pastoral care in the community entrusted to him under the authority of the diocesan bishop in whose ministry of Christ he has been called to share." But he does this "with the cooperation of other presbyters or deacons and the assistance of lay members of the Christian faithful" (Code of Canon Law, #519). In other words, it's a communal ministry. As "official shepherd" the pastor has to answer publicly for the care of the flock. But the lay members are committed, just as much as the pastor is, to caring for the flock. They just do it in different ways. And they, too, must "answer" for the sheep. They answer privately to Jesus Christ, the Good Shepherd, to whom all of us who have promised to "love one another as he has loved us" must constantly answer for the love we show to others. What Jesus said to Peter he says to all, "If you love me, feed my sheep."

The law of love is the law of ministry. To love is to care for others, to "have concern for the sheep," and not abandon them when we see the wolf coming, or because other things are more important to us. Jesus says, "A good shepherd lays down his life for the sheep." That is the measure of the care we should have for each other and of the priority we should give to ministering to one another as priests.

Reflecting on This Week's Gospels

Fourth Week of Easter

Pray daily: Lord Jesus, you have called me to "lay down my life" for your sheep. Give me the love to do this by taking up my life daily in care and concern for those whom you love.

Monday: John 10:1-10. "I came that they might have life, and have it abundantly." Can you say that you live so that others might have life—the divine life of God, which you are empowered to give them?

Tuesday: John 10:22-30. "My sheep hear my voice; I know them, and they follow me." Whom do you know who does not appear to be following Jesus completely? How have you let that person hear Jesus' voice through you?

Wednesday: John 12:44-50. "I came as light into the world, so that everyone who believes in me should not remain in the darkness." Do you know anyone who seems to be in "darkness" where you work? In your home? In your social life? What are you doing to share Christ's light in you?

Thursday: John 13:16-20. "Very truly, I tell you, servants are not greater than their master, nor are messengers greater than the one who sent them." Do you require respect and gratitude as a condition for ministering to others?

Friday: John 14:1-6. Jesus said, "I am the way, and the truth, and the life. No one comes to the Father except through me." If you know the way, and the truth, how are you helping those who do not?

Saturday: John 14:7-14. "Very truly, I tell you, the one who believes in me will also do the works that I do and, in fact, will do greater works than these." What can Jesus do in you and through you that is "greater" than what he did in the body he was born with?

Living This Week's Gospels

As Christian: Try to identify what seems to be the "way" for people you live or work or recreate with. What do they accept as truth? What is fulfillment in life for them? Compare this to Jesus as the Way, the Truth, the Life.

As Disciple: Read Matthew 5:21-28, asking how believing and living this could solve some problems of specific people you know.

As Prophet: Change something in your life-style for the sake of making some truth or value more evident to someone you know.

As Priest: Ask who first comes to mind when you think of "lost sheep." Take one step in action toward helping or healing that person.

As King: Ask what, in your own environment, is making it hard for people to live in conscious union with Jesus Christ. Do one thing toward changing this.

Fifth Sunday of Easter

Priests Pray as Christ

Acts 9:26-31; 1 John 3:18-24; John 15:1-8

T he key to all priestly ministry—both of priests by Holy Orders and of priests by Baptism—is union with Christ. Jesus said, "Those who abide in me and I in them bear much fruit."

Jesus rose to live multiplied in all of us who by Baptism would "offer our bodies as a living sacrifice to God" to become his Body. In us and through our human actions he continues his human presence and ministry on earth. Because of our union with Christ in grace, our actions are not just human, but also divine. They are Christ's actions as well as ours. That is why they can produce divine results.

A branch "cannot bear fruit by itself unless it abides in the vine." That is why Jesus says, "Apart from me you can do nothing." The first thing we must do if we want to minister as "priests in the Priest" is seek deeper union of mind and heart and will with Jesus Christ. That is why Jesus associates bearing fruit with discipleship, or the effort to grow in union with him: "By this is my Father glorified, that you bear much fruit and become my disciples."

The path to union with Jesus goes through his words. His words reveal his mind to us; his words speak to our hearts; we make choices with our wills in response to his words— both the words he spoke verbally and the words he lived out in action. To be a disciple is to live a life characterized by reflection on his words. And so Jesus said, "If you abide in me and my words abide in you, ask for whatever you wish and it will be done for you."

When we pray as the body of Christ, Jesus prays, and his prayers are heard. There are two ways to pray as the body of Christ: The first is for the Church to pray publicly, officially, in liturgy and sacraments. The presence of an ordained minister (priest or deacon) speaking as a representative of the Church in visible union with the bishop says that the whole Church is speaking or praying. And Jesus has pledged (*sacrament* means "pledge") that he himself will be speaking in his Body. That is why the sacraments always effect what they signify.

We also pray as the Body of Christ when we pray in union with his Spirit. And the surest sign that we are in fact praying by the Spirit of Christ is that we are living out our faith in love, striving to do everything Jesus commanded. "Beloved, if our hearts do not condemn us we have boldness before God; and we receive from him whatever we ask, because we... believe in the name of his Son Jesus Christ and love one another just as he has commanded us." This is our assurance that we are in union with Christ through his Spirit: "All who obey his commandments abide in him, and he abides in them."

Jesus the priest prayed for his people. And as his Body on earth we are a priestly people commissioned by him to pray in his name for one another, for the Church, and for the whole world. This is our priestly office, a sacred function entrusted to each one of us and to all of us communally as a community of priests. When we pray together officially it is a priest or deacon named by the Church who leads us. But when any Christian baptized into the priesthood of Jesus Christ prays, whether publicly or privately, that is an exercise of priesthood to which he or she was commissioned by Jesus himself. Every prayer we offer is in his name.

The greatest prayer we can offer for anyone or anything is the Mass: the prayer of offering the Body and Blood of Jesus, and ourselves with him and in him, for the life of the world. Any time we participate in the Eucharistic celebration, we do so as priests, joining in the prayer as priests. This is a reason, not only to participate in the Sunday celebration, when all God's priestly people are called to pray for the world, but in daily Mass as well.

Reflecting on This Week's Gospels

Fifth Week of Easter

Pray daily: Lord Jesus, you have called me into the intimate union of sharing your life and your mission on earth. Fill my mind with your thoughts, my heart with your love, that I might fill the world with your presence.

Monday: John 14:21-26. "Those who love me will keep my word, and my Father will love them, and we will come to them and make our dwelling with them." How can you remain conscious all day that God loves you and is dwelling inside of you?

Tuesday: John 14:27-31. "Peace I leave with you; my peace I give to you. I do not give to you as the world gives. Do not let your hearts be troubled, and do not let them be afraid." Do you cultivate deep peace in your heart through prayer so that you might radiate peace, and give peace to others?

Wednesday: John 15:1-8. "My Father glorified by this, that you bear much fruit and become my disciples." What do you see as the fruit of your life as a priest? Are you dedicated to discipleship as a priest?

Thursday: John 15:9-11. "As the Father has loved me, so I have loved you; abide in my love." How often do you sit quietly and try to absorb the fact and the way God loves you?

Friday: John 15:12-17. "You are my friends if you do what I command you." Have you experienced intimate union with Jesus Christ by trying to minister as his Body?

Saturday: John 15:18-21. "If you belonged to the world, the world would love you as its own. Because you do not belong to the world, but I have chosen you out of the world—therefore the world hates you." What experience have you had of being a victim with Christ by trying to minister as a priest with Christ.

Living This Week's Gospels

As Christian: Respond to any bad news you hear by praying in the name of Jesus, conscious of your consecration as priest.

As Disciple: Commit yourself to "in service" training as a priest: make a retreat, enroll in a class or discussion group, give time daily to discipleship.

As Prophet: Scan your life-style, looking for anything not in harmony with your consecration as a priest.

As Priest: Consciously, with deliberate faith and love, pray for the world at Mass and alone, drawing hope from your commission to do this in Christ's name as a priest.

As King: Take responsibility for lifting up to God in prayer anything you see in society which needs to be changed. Train yourself to react to evil and injustice as a priest, with hope, compassion, love and an immediate turning to God in prayer.

Sixth Sunday of Easter

Priests Give Life in Love

Acts 10:25-26, 34-35, 44-48; 1 John 4:7-10; John 15:9-17

What, in a nutshell, is priesthood? It is to give life to others by giving our lives in love. This is what Jesus came to do as priest; it is what we are consecrated to do by Baptism. "God sent his only Son into the world so that we might live through him." "This is my commandment, that you love one another as I have loved you. No one has greater love than this, to lay down one's life for one's friends."

This is not an abstract definition of priesthood. It is the definition of the concrete, specific priesthood of Jesus Christ, which is the only real priesthood that exists. And all of us who are "in Christ," all who are members of his Body by Baptism, are "priests in the Priest." We are also "victims in the Victim," because the sacrifice Jesus offered as Priest was his own body, his life.

Jesus gave his life so that we, as many grains of wheat, might be mixed into one dough by the water of Baptism and baked into one bread by the fire of the Holy Spirit (breviary reading, Second Thursday of Easter). The life he died to give us is not just individual, private life; it is a sharing together in the life of God, a sharing which also makes us one with each other. The Christian life is a shared life, which is why the choice to enter into life is a choice to enter into community. This is why the priesthood which gives life is a priesthood which builds and serves community.

In God and in the Church, "life" and "love" and "light" are used interchangeably. John writes, "Everyone who loves is begotten by God and knows God." Jesus said, "I am the way, the truth and the life." The way is love. The way of love is truth. Love and truth are the life of God. They are our life in God, in Christ. But love is not love until it is given to another. Truth is not truth until it is expressed to another. And for Christians life is not life unless it is union with God and with others in Christ. Priesthood, then, serves truth, love and life fostered in community.

Priests serve truth by communicating the word of God; they serve life by ministries which heal and make holy; they serve love by all that forms people into community. Ordained priests "teach, sanctify and govern" with the authority required by their responsibility as public, official ministers in the Church. Non-ordained priests (all the baptized) have the same responsibility to foster truth, life and love in the community in private, personal ways. They teach by all they say and do. They heal and make holy by their every prayer for others, especially by their priestly participation in liturgy, and by their loving concern and care for others. They achieve the end of government (unity, peace, the common good) by all they do to foster community in their families, in their professional and social circles, within their parishes, the Church and the world.

To be a priest is to give one's life for this, which is to give one's life to this. To accept Baptism is already to "lay down one's life for the sheep," because by Baptism we accepted to die in Christ: to die to life limited to human dimensions and to live a new life, the divine life of Jesus as his body on earth. We "offered our bodies as a living sacrifice" to continue his presence, his mission, his ministry on earth. Now it is "no longer just we who live, but Christ lives in us." Our lives are not our own; we have died and our lives are hidden with Christ in God. All of us who were baptized into Christ have clothed ourselves with Christ. We see it as infidelity whenever we seek our own interests, not those of Jesus Christ.

In Eucharist, all present offer themselves to be, with and in Christ, "the bread of life." And each says with Jesus, "The bread that I give is my flesh for the life of the world." To live this is to live the priesthood of Jesus Christ.

Reflecting on This Week's Gospels

Sixth Week of Easter

Pray daily: Jesus, you are the Lamb of God. You offer yourself constantly for the life of the world. Through Eucharist conform my heart and my life to yours. Teach me to offer my life constantly in life-giving love.

Monday: John 15:26 to 16:4. "When the Advocate comes whom I will send to you from the Father, the Spirit of truth who comes from the Father, he will testify on my behalf." God gives us life through the gift of the Spirit. How do you, can you, share that Spirit with others?

Tuesday: John 16:5-11. "[I]t is to your advantage that I go away, for if I do not go away, the Advocate will not come to you; but if I go, I will send him to you." Why is the presence of the Spirit in our hearts better for us than Christ's visible presence in the flesh?

Wednesday: John 16:12-15: "When the Spirit of truth comes, he will guide you into all truth." What do you need to do, on your part, to experience the Spirit teaching you?

Ascension Thursday: Mark 16:15-20: He said to them, "Go into all the world and proclaim the good news to the whole creation. The one who believes and is baptized will be saved...." Do you really believe that you can help give people life for all eternity by sharing with them what you know of the Gospel?

Friday: John 16:20-23: "When a woman is in labor, she has pain, because her hour has come. But when her child is born, she no longer remembers the anguish because of the joy of having brought a human being into the world." What would it cost you to be "in labor" giving eternal life to others? Have you experienced the joy of this?

Saturday: John 16:23-28. "Until now you have not asked for anything in my name. Ask and you will receive, so that your joy may be complete." What does it mean to ask "in Jesus' name"? Does it mean to ask as his Body, given entirely in love for others? Are your prayers characterized by desire that you and others should have the fullness of life Jesus came to give?

Living This Week's Gospels

As Christian: Spend three minutes thinking about the awesome power you have to save lives for all eternity. How do you use it?

As Disciple: Each day jot down one thing Jesus has shared with you that says you are his friend?

As Prophet: What in your life-style would let people know that you are a priest?

As Priest: Do one thing to "induce labor" so that you might help another be born into eternal life. For example, begin a relationship, invite someone to Mass, share a book, ask a question.

As King: Do you have any kind of authority over any people? Are you responsible for exercising it as a "royal priesthood?" Ask how you could.

Seventh Sunday of Easter

Priests Are a Sign

Acts 1:15-17, 20-26; 1 John 4:11-16; John 17:11-19

A ny priest leading people in worship of a transcendent God expresses the community's recognition that they do not simply "belong to the world"—that they are at least in relationship with a Being who is not just from and of this world.

Christian priesthood, however, is precisely a witness to the Resurrection of Jesus Christ. Whether we are priests by Baptism only or by Holy Orders as well, we minister to make the risen, living Jesus visibly present in word, in sacrament and in community.

We are all equipped as priests for the work of ministry, for building up the Body of Christ, which is the community of the Church. Ordained priests do this officially, receiving from the bishop the public responsibility of pastors and the authority to act in his name. Non-ordained priests are just as responsible for building up the Body of Christ, but they exercise their ministry in private, personal ways or as participating in the public ministry of the parish under the authority of the pastor.

The community Christians form is a Eucharistic community. Priests in Holy Orders are ordained specifically to preside at the Eucharistic celebration, which expresses the triumph of Jesus sacrificed and risen to be for all time the Bread of Life for all who believe. Their presence is necessary to form the local church as a Eucharistic, sacramental community. Vatican II taught that "the liturgy is the summit toward which all the activity of the Church is directed... and the fountain from which all her power flows" *(Constitution on the Sacred Liturgy,* #10). A Church without ordained priests and Eucharist is like a body on a life-support system, being kept alive by the extraordinary intervention of God. Eucharist is the unambiguous sign of belief in Jesus risen and present.

Participation in Eucharist is only possible for those who by Baptism are members of the risen Christ, because only the body of Christ can offer itself as victim and priest with Christ and in Christ at Mass. And only those who live by the life of Christ as his Body can receive the Bread which nourishes divine, not human, life. Eucharist, then, makes visible the presence of the risen Jesus in the Church. And to participate in Eucharist, whether as a priest by Baptism or by ordination as well, is an act of Christian priesthood that bears witness to the Resurrection of Jesus.

The ordained priest makes Jesus present on the altar at Mass, not because he has been given some personal power to do so, but because in union with the whole congregation he asks God officially in the name of the Church to do it: "Father, we bring you these gifts. We ask you to make them holy by the power of your Spirit, that they may become the body and blood of your Son, our Lord Jesus Christ." This prayer is always answered because it is the prayer of Jesus himself speaking in and through his Church. The power given to the ordained priest is the power to preside publicly and officially at liturgy in the name of the bishop so that it will be the sacramental prayer of the whole Church.

All of us who, with the presider, ask God to change the bread and wine into the Body and Blood of Christ are by that very fact asking God, "Bring the image of your Son to perfection within us" (Lent, Preface I). We are offering ourselves in and with Christ to be changed, to be perfectly his Body, to be offered and given like him, the Lamb of God, "so that sins may be forgiven." We are offering our lives, our time on this earth, our "flesh, for the life of the world." This is priesthood.

And this is a clear expression that we do not "belong to this world." It is a commitment to live out the words of Jesus, to express in action a spirit that is not of this world. To be a priest is to be a witness, "consecrated in truth."

Reflecting on This Week's Gospels

Seventh Week of Easter

Pray daily: Jesus, you have consecrated me to the priesthood of expressing your presence, your truth, your love. Live in me, and through me give life to the world.

Monday: John 16:29-33. "In the world you face persecution. But take courage; I have conquered the world!" Do you live and act as one who believes this? How, specifically, do you draw strength from knowing Jesus overcame both sin and death?

Tuesday: John 17:1-11: "Glorify your son, so that the son may glorify you." How did Jesus glorify the Father—that is, make him look good? How can you glorify Jesus? How and you show he is risen and living in you?

Wednesday: John 17:11-19: "As you have sent me into the world, so I sent them into the world." What has Jesus sent you to do? What would you like it to be? Are you, or could you be, doing it right now?

Thursday: John 17:20-26: "I ask not only on behalf of these, but also on behalf of those who will believe in me through their word." Who has come to believe in Christ more through your words, spoken or embodied in action?

Friday: John 21:15-19: "Simon son of John, do you love me?" Peter responded, "Yes, Lord; you know that I love you." Jesus said to him, "Tend my sheep." How have you shown your love for Christ by ministering to others? How could you?

Saturday: John 21:20-25: "There are also many other things that Jesus did; if every one of them were written down, I suppose that world itself could not contain the books that would be written." As priest and witness, how much of Jesus' story are you familiar enough with to share it with others? What opportunities exist for you to learn more? To share what you know with others?

Living This Week's Gospels

As Christian: Reexamine your priorities. What takes precedence in your life over a chance to offer and to receive the Body and Blood of Christ at Mass?

As Disciple: Read through one of the Eucharistic Prayers of the Mass, noticing what the presider says in your name.

As Prophet: Identify something in your life-style which says you do not "belong to the world."

As Priest: Consciously offer to God everything you touch during the day, just as you offer the bread and wine at Mass, asking that it be consecrated to doing the work of God.

As King: Is there any change you can accomplish or urge in your family, social or professional environment which would counteract the tendency we have to go along as if we only belonged to this world?

Pentecost

Priests Speak

Acts 2:1-11; 1 Corinthians 12:3-7, 12-13; John 20:19-23

W hen the community of believers had assembled for the Jewish feast of Pentecost, it was in the form of tongues of fire that the Holy Spirit came down upon them. And the first effect of this was that they began to speak, to express themselves.

This was appropriate. Before his Ascension, Jesus had told the eleven apostles, "Go into the whole world and proclaim the good news to all creation. Penance for the remission of sins is to be preached. You are to be my witnesses, even to the ends of the earth. Go, make disciples of all the nations. Teach them."

These instructions echo the repeated description of Jesus' own ministry on earth: he "went about... teaching... and proclaiming the good news... and curing" (Matthew 5:23, 9:35). The apostles are to go into the whole world to teach, to proclaim and to heal by forgiving sins.

Public, official responsibility for this ministry is given to the apostles, and with this responsibility they receive the authority that must accompany it. This is the public responsibility and authority that is passed down through the sacrament of Holy Orders to bishops and to the clergy associated with them.

The Spirit, however, is given, not just to ordained priests, but to all who are priests through Baptism. In his Pentecost sermon, Peter proclaims the fulfillment of God's promise: "In the last days it will be, God declares, / that I will pour out my Spirit upon all flesh, / and your sons and your daughters shall prophesy, / and your young men shall see visions, / and your old men shall dream dreams. / Even upon my slaves, both men and women, / in those days I will pour out my Spirit; / and they shall prophesy."

To be a Christian, then, is to be chosen and sent by God to speak by word and action: to "go into the whole world," the world of family and social life, of business and politics, and there to "teach" and "proclaim" and "cure." For this the Holy Spirit is given to every baptized member of the Church. And the Spirit is given to be visible, to be expressed in each one: To each individual the manifestation of the Spirit is given for the common good.

To not express the Spirit is to stifle the Spirit. Suppose that after the tongues of flame came to rest on all those assembled on the day of Pentecost any one of them had copped out, claiming to be too embarrassed or afraid to stand up and say anything. Suppose that any one of us, after receiving the Holy Spirit at Baptism and Confirmation, claims to be too embarrassed to proclaim the good news at home, at school or at work? Suppose we are afraid to teach by challenging the attitudes and values around us? Suppose we refuse to heal by going out to others with merciful, ministering love? Can we who are marked with tongues of fire cower, cold and mute, in silence?

Pentecost means "the fiftieth day" after Passover. It coincided with the Jewish feast of first fruits, of thanksgiving for the harvest, the Feast of Weeks. As a time of joy and reward, it was an image of God's final judgment. And since on Pentecost, as on the feasts of Passover and Booths, Jews went on pilgrimage to Jerusalem, it was later seen as a memorial of the Covenant, when God gave the Law on Sinai.

The Christian feast is all of these things. On Pentecost the Church was born and the new Covenant of Spirit rather than Law was proclaimed. Those who received the Holy Spirit were the "first fruits" of redemption and a preview of the "harvest" Jesus sent his disciples to gather (Matthew 9:37). The gift of the Spirit was a judgment passed on all who thought Christ had failed (John 16:8). And as priests we are sent to proclaim this with tongues of fire.

Reflecting on This Week's Gospels

Note: *You will need to check the Liturgical Calendar on page x to find out what week of the year follows Pentecost Sunday this year. Once you know which week it is, you can find the weekday Gospel reflections after that week's Sunday Gospel reflection. For example, if the week following Pentecost Sunday is the Tenth Week of the Year, then locate the Tenth Sunday of the Year and the weekday reflections for the Tenth Week will follow.*

ORDINARY TIME

Tenth Sunday of the Year Through Thirty-Fourth Sunday of the Year

Tenth Sunday of the Year

The Heart of It All

Genesis 3:9-15; 2 Corinthians 4:13 to 5:1; Mark 3:20-35

Devotion to Christ's Heart is "Christian spirituality in a nutshell" (Pope Pius XII). This devotion can be summed up in three words: adoration, reparation, consecration—with Christ's flesh-and-blood, divine humanity as the focus of them all.

When Jesus teaches we must be undivided in our loyalty to him, and have no other god, no other focus of our hearts except him, this is the core of adoration, of devotion to the Sacred Heart and of Christianity itself: to love God with our whole hearts.

Many people refuse to love, or to express love, because love makes us vulnerable to the pain of rejection. By offering himself visibly to us in his humanity, and by speaking explicit words of teaching and invitation, God made himself vulnerable to explicit, visible rejection. The love of God made visible in Jesus as it never was before also made sin visible in the world as never before. This calls for visible "reparation," for visible expression of our love for God in response to the visible reality of sin.

Reparation and forgiveness go together. The reparation which Jesus made on the cross was by its very nature also an act of forgiveness. We cannot make reparation for sin while rejecting those who reject God—or us. The Our Father reminds us we cannot even ask for forgiveness without forgiving—or asking for the grace to forgive. We call confession "the Sacrament of Reconciliation," because in this act we are reconciled both with God and with other people. We are forgiven and we forgive. "Communal Reconciliation" services bring this out: They are a united, visible profession that we all renounce the sins which divide us from God and from one another.

The message of the Gospel is that "in Christ God was reconciling the world to himself, not counting their trespasses against them, and entrusting the message of reconciliation to us" (see 2 Corinthians 5:19). To do what Jesus died for is to make reparation for sin. It is also to bring about healing. The real wounds of the world, or of any human heart, are not the lesions of the flesh that cause loss of blood and bring about the disintegration of the body. They are the hurtful acts which cause loss of trust and bring about division between individuals and nations, the disintegration of society. And modern prophets from three different religions—Ghandi, Martin Luther King and Thomas Merton—are united in proclaiming that only forgiveness, given prior to justice, can heal this disintegration.

Paul preached that the purpose of Jesus' coming was "to gather up all things in him, things in heaven and things on earth" under his reign (Ephesians 1:10). The word *community* means a "common unity." Whenever we celebrate together—"communally"—our common unity of faith, hope and love, our common unity in the act of adoring, making reparation, expressing forgiveness and accepting forgiveness, we are expressing our "common unity" of consecration to the goal of Christ's coming.

Consecration means "dedication," being given and set aside for something or someone in particular. To "consecrate" ourselves to the heart of Christ is to recognize the desire of his heart and dedicate ourselves to fulfilling it. And the desire of his heart is to bring everything and everybody on earth together in love in the unity of his Body, his Church, his shared life. We can see and hear and feel this desire in the Gospel scene when Jesus glanced around the circle of those seated around him and said, "These are my mother and brothers! Whoever does the will of God is brother and sister and mother to me." When we can say the same, we will know we have accepted our baptismal consecration to bringing about the desire of his heart: the unity of the human race in the life and family of God. To do this is to share Christ's mission and his heart.

Reflecting on This Week's Gospels

Tenth Week of the Year

> *Pray daily: Lord, I believe that you are the Lord and Savior of the world, and no power of evil can stand against you. Teach me to stand with you at every moment of my day, so that no fear will have power over me.*

Monday: Matthew 5:1-12. "Blessed are those who hunger and thirst for righteousness, for they will be filled." Do you hunger for Eucharist, the holiness of God incarnate given to you as food and gift? Is this a hunger you can foster in yourself?

Tuesday: Matthew 5:13-16. "You are the salt of the earth; but if salt has lost its taste, how can its saltiness be restored? ...You are the light of the world." Do you believe Eucharist can season you with the taste of Christ? Does the desire to be salt and light for others motivate you to nourish yourself with word and sacrament?

Wednesday: Matthew 5:17-19. "[W]hoever does them [obeys these commandments] and teaches them will be called great in the kingdom of heaven." Do you focus as much on teaching Christ's way as on following it?

Thursday: Matthew 5:20-26. "[W]hen you are offering your gift at the altar, if you remember that your brother or sister has anything against you...go; first be reconciled...." At every Eucharist, do you consciously commit yourself to love as Christ does? Do you ask help?

Friday: Matthew 5:27-32. "You have heard that it was said, 'You shall not commit adultery.' But I say to you, everyone who looks at a woman with lust has already committed adultery with her in his heart." Are you conscious of your sacredness as the Body of Christ? Of the sacredness of every other person who is Christ's Body?

Saturday: Matthew 5:33-37. "[D]o not swear by your head, for you cannot make a single hair white or black. Let your word be 'Yes, Yes,' or 'No, No'; anything more than this comes from the evil one." As the Body of Christ, are you conscious that every word you speak should be worthy of Christ himself?

Living This Week's Gospels

As Christian: Put something visible in your house or room which proclaims that Jesus is Lord there. Look at it consciously every time you come in or go out.

As Disciple: How many explicit instances can you remember or identify when Jesus clearly protected you from something?

As Prophet: Look around your house, and at the space you control at work: Is there anything visible which hints at a divided loyalty? Does anything express acceptance of values contrary to those Jesus taught?

As Priest: Each time you go to work, go shopping, or come into contact with other people, say with Jesus, "These are my family: whoever does the will of God is brother and sister to me."

As King: Look at any problem you have been afraid to address. Think consciously about Christ's power to cast out Satan and overcome evil. Take courage and act.

Eleventh Sunday of the Year

The Gift of Understanding

Ezekiel 17:22-24; 2 Corinthians 5:6-10; Mark 4:26-34

God sent the Holy Spirit into the Church to make the seeds planted by Jesus grow. Through the Spirit people are gifted in different ways "for the work of ministry, for building up the body of Christ, until all of us come to...the full stature of Christ...from whom the whole body, joined and knit together by every ligament with which it is equipped, as each part is working properly, promotes the body's growth in building itself up in love" (Ephesians 4:11-16).

This means that our image of the Church should be a community of growth and change, a Church in which continuing discipleship and clarification of understanding leads constantly to prophetic insights and new initiatives. Except for essential characteristics, the Church today should no more look or act like the Church we grew up in or the Church at the time of the twelve apostles than a bush looks like a seed.

To understand this is to understand what is wrong with the Protestant insistence on finding everything in the Bible. The Church was in such bad shape in the sixteenth century that those who became Protestants just could not believe that the Holy Spirit could guarantee that a community of live human beings (which means sinful human beings) would pass down the teaching of Jesus faithfully until the end of time. They withdrew their faith from the Church and put it in the Bible instead. People change; words written in a book do not. The basis of Protestantism is the refusal to believe that the Spirit who inspired some human beings to write the Bible could keep a designated group of human beings (the hierarchy, the official teachers in the Church) faithful forever in interpreting the Bible in spite of their sinfulness. They rely instead on the interpretation of private individuals who show signs of holiness.

We follow this same principle, consciously or not, when we want to have the teaching of the Church fixed and untouchable in the words of some "final version" of the catechism which will provide a sure and certain norm for our belief and silence all controversies forever. It makes one think of Hitler's "final solution" to what he called "the Jewish problem." When life becomes a problem to us, we kill. When the live presence of the Spirit in the Church becomes a problem to us, we try to put the Spirit to death—unaware that in doing so we are destroying our own spirits as well.

This same refusal to trust in the Spirit's action in the Church makes us want to cling to the past, to what we are used to. Every change is risky. There is danger of error. We forget that there is even more danger in not changing, in remaining stable and stagnant when the Spirit is trying to "lift high the lowly tree...and make the withered tree bloom." When Hitler tried to resolve the "Jewish problem" by killing the Jews, he created the "Nazi problem." If we try to resolve the problem of "false prophets" in the Church by killing the Spirit, we multiply the problem Jesus had most trouble with, the "Pharisee problem."

The Holy Spirit gives the gift of understanding, which enables us to perceive clearly the meaning and the truthfulness of Christ's teaching. It is not a quality (like, for example, the ability to read) given once and for all that is ours to apply at will. The gift of understanding is inseparable from the abiding, active presence of the Holy Spirit. Both in individuals and in the Church, understanding of the faith grows from day to day and down through the centuries as we learn from the Spirit. The value of "tradition" in the Church, which Catholics accept with Scripture as a norm of faith, is that it passes on to each new generation the understanding of Christ's teaching acquired by the passing generation in its turn. To be faithful to the Spirit we, in our time, must use the gift of understanding to see, to change and to grow.

Reflecting on This Week's Gospels

Eleventh Week of the Year

Pray daily: Lord, you gave us your Spirit to abide with us, teach us and guide us. Give us the trust that will free us to follow the Spirit's voice.

Monday: Matthew 5:38-42. "You have heard that it was said, 'An eye for an eye and a tooth for a tooth.' But I say to you...." How many things can you name that Jesus changed in the religion God taught the Chosen People?

Tuesday: Matthew 5:43-48. "Be perfect, therefore, as your heavenly Father is perfect." Does Jesus expect us, or the Church, to be perfect immediately? How does this affect your attitude toward constant changes in the Church?

Wednesday: Matthew 6:1-6, 16-18. "Beware of practicing your piety before others in order to be seen." Why do people approve when we perform traditional religious acts? Why do new expressions of devotion or decisions in faith upset them?

Thursday: Matthew 6:7-15. "Pray then in this way: Our Father... give us this day our daily bread." What attitude toward security does this prayer form in us?

Friday: Matthew 6:19-23. "The eye is the lamp of the body. So, if your eye is healthy, your whole body will be full of light." How can we be sure the "lamp" of our spiritual vision is sound? What happens if we just distrust it and live by external rules?

Saturday: Matthew 6:24-34. "Therefore I tell you, do not worry about your life, what you will eat...or about your body, what you will wear." Could this teaching ever be embodied in Church rules or laws? Has our understanding of it grown over the years?

Living This Week's Gospels

As Christian: On a scale of one to ten, grade how much trust you have in the Holy Spirit's guidance of the Church through each of the following: pope, bishops, priests, laity in general and yourself. What does this tell you about yourself?

As Disciple: Identify one Scripture text about which you have a special insight or understanding. If you cannot think of one, read the Gospels reflectively until you have one.

As Prophet: Name three things in your life-style or behavior that show you are led personally by the Spirit in addition to Church rules and practices. Try to add one.

As Priest: Ask how you have accepted Vatican II's encouragement of lay ministry. How could you convert more to this teaching?

As King: What changes have you tried to make in the way your family lives? In the policies people follow at work? In the practices of your social group? What changes could you make? (Begin with one and try it.)

The Gift of Awe or Fear of the Lord

Job 38:1, 8-11; 2 Corinthians 5:14-17; Mark 4:35-41

God sent the Holy Spirit to fill the Church with the same sense of awe and faith that filled the boat where the disciples were when Jesus quieted the wind and the sea. The Spirit makes manifest the presence, power and mystery of God (see Acts 2:2).

This "awe" is "fear of the Lord," and it is one of the gifts of the Holy Spirit. Fear to us seems negative; we associate it with being "scared" of God when we were little. But if we ask what fear is minus the emotion of fright, we get perspective. By "fear of the Lord" we see God in perspective, and we see the immensity of God's power, God's goodness, God's love compared with those of any creature.

If we see God's power in a context of being threatened by some created power—as the disciples were threatened by the storm and the Church by persecution—then "fear of the Lord" is comforting. The more awe we feel at the presence and power of God, the less fear we have of anything mere human beings or natural forces can do to us. To walk with that fear of the Lord which is the Spirit's gift of awe is roughly like the feeling one has when walking down a dark street with a hundred-and-fifty-pound Doberman at one's side. It is awesomely reassuring.

When evil and pain are a mystery to us, as they were to Job, and we cannot comprehend how God can permit suffering, the Holy Spirit gives us a sense of awe at the incomprehensible scope and mystery of God's knowledge, God's wisdom compared to ours. "The LORD answered Job out of the whirlwind: 'Who is this that darkens divine counsel by words without knowledge? / Gird up your loins like a man, / I will question you, and you shall declare to me. / Where were you when I laid the foundation of the earth? / Tell me, if you have understanding. / Who determined its measurements—surely you know! / ...who laid the cornerstone, / when the morning stars sang together / and all the heavenly beings shouted for joy? / Or who shut in the sea with doors / when it burst out from the womb? / ...Have you commanded the morning since your days began, / and caused the dawn to know its place? / ...Have the gates of death been revealed to you? / ...Declare, if you know all!'" The gift of awe puts God's knowledge and ours in perspective. It does not give us answers, but it takes away the arrogance which makes us think our own way of seeing things is the answer.

The Holy Spirit also fills us with awe and wonder as we see each other with new eyes. As Saint Paul says, "From now on...we regard no one from a human point of view.... if anyone is in Christ, there is a new creation." Every one of us who shares in the life of God by grace is the Body of Christ, a child of God, a temple of the Holy Spirit. The "manifestation of the Spirit" through the community's expressions of faith, hope and love, and through the visible exercise of each one's gifts of ministry, makes manifest the presence, power and mystery of God in the congregation, in the Church.

Sometimes Jesus embodied and visible in the actions of his Body on earth seems to be asleep during times of crisis or need in the world, or in our ordinary experience of liturgy, or of the Church's ministry. When those members of the Church who should be most responsive seem to be "asleep," oblivious of the needs of the times, we feel like going to Jesus, saying, "Teacher, do you not care that we are perishing?" And we should do this. We should speak up to bishops, pastors, politicians, teachers, business people, parents, students and children, shaking each other awake. And we should speak to Jesus in prayer; but with faith, not doubting; asking the Spirit for such a sense of the awesome power of love God has unleashed on earth that our panic will turn into a "great calm" that allows us to return to our oars and concentrate on rowing.

Reflecting on This Week's Gospels

Twelfth Week of the Year

Pray daily: Lord, you kept saying to your disciples, "Do not be afraid." Give me such an awe of your power that I will fear nothing on earth again.

Monday: Matthew 7:1-5. "For with the judgment you make you will be judged, and the measure you give will be the measure you get." In your judgments about the Church and others, what changes, if you include in your measurements the presence of the Holy Spirit and God's power?

Tuesday: Matthew 7:6, 12-14. "Do not give what is holy to dogs; and do not throw your pearls before swine, or they will trample them underfoot and turn and maul you." Should you expect, without deep faith, to understand what is expressed in liturgy, God's laws, Church teaching? Do you ever get hostile because you do not understand?

Wednesday: Matthew 7:15-20. "You will know them by their fruits. Are grapes gathered from thorns, or figs from thistles?" What awesome signs of holiness do you see in the Church (for example: saints, ideals)?

Thursday: Matthew 7:21-29. "[T]he crowds were astounded at his teaching, for he taught them as one having authority, and not as their scribes." How awesome is it that the Church has preserved Jesus' teaching intact for two thousand years?

Friday: Matthew 8:1-4. When Jesus came down from the mountain... a leper approached, did him homage, and said, "Lord, if you choose, you can make me clean." When you approach Jesus in prayer, what is your attitude toward him? If the leper had just seen Jesus transfigured as the disciples had, would his have been different?

Saturday: Matthew 8:5-17. The centurion said in reply, "Lord, I am not worthy to have you come under my roof;

but only speak the word, and my servant will be healed."
How much awe should you have when you receive
Communion? What fosters it?

Living This Week's Gospels

As Christian: List your three greatest fears. Ask how Jesus
saves you from them. Do some act that expresses trust in his
power with regard to each one.

As Disciple: Reflect on what is good and bad about fear.
How is "fear of the Lord" different from being afraid
of God?

As Prophet: Overcome your fear of being different in some
act which expresses the attitudes or values taught by Jesus.

As Priest: Examine how careful you are about showing
reverence in church; for example, genuflecting or bowing
whenever you pass in front of the Blessed Sacrament. How
does your body language affect others?

As King: Ask what you could change in policies or customs
where you live, work or recreate which do not express
authentic reverence for what human persons are. What does
respect seem to be based on? On what should it be based?

Thirteenth Sunday of the Year

The Gift of Courage or Fortitude

Wisdom 1:13-15; 2:23-24; 2 Corinthians 8:7, 9, 13-15;
Mark 5:21-43

God sent the Holy Spirit to fill the Church with that courage to which Jesus exhorted his disciples when he said, "Take courage, I have conquered the world." The Church is to be a community without fear of rejection by others, of poverty, or of death itself; a community free to live on the level of God, confident in its power to give divine life through the ministry of word, witness and sacrament.

To be healed by Jesus, like the woman afflicted with hemorrhages, we have to be brave enough to stand up and step out from the crowd, to risk ridicule and rejection. It is the Holy Spirit who empowers us to do this, as Jesus recognized when he said to the woman, "Daughter, your faith has made you well; go in peace and be healed of your disease." The courage which comes from faith is not the courage of this world. It is a gift of the Holy Spirit.

Jesus himself gave us an example of freedom from slavery to cultural prejudices and assumptions when he risked (and got) ridicule for disregarding the message that the girl he was on the way to cure had already died. Christians should act over and over again like people who never got the message the culture is constantly delivering. Christ's message is the one to which we listen and by which we live, and it is a message of life, not death; and of freedom to live life "to the full," not restricted only to those hopes and possibilities that are attainable within the narrow dimensions of this world.

We know that "God did not make death, / and he does not delight in the death of the living. For he created all things so that they might exist; / the generative forces of the world are wholesome, / ... God created us for incorruption, / and made us in the image of his own eternity." We know that nothing in this world can keep us from everlasting life, and that is the wellspring of our courage to break with the despairing priorities of this world.

The gift of courage is also the source of Christian generosity. Christians have no fear of poverty; much less do they place any value on affluence. As a result, they are free to share what they have with others generously, without the paralyzing anxiety which comes from worrying about "What are we to eat?" or "What are we to drink?" or "What are we to wear?" They know their heavenly Father knows what they need, and that if they "seek first the kingdom of God" and live in love for God and others, all that they need will be given them besides (see Matthew 6:31-33).

Saint Paul holds before the eyes of the Corinthians, from whom he was seeking financial help for the Church in Jerusalem, the example of Jesus: "For you know the generous act of our Lord Jesus Christ, that though he was rich, yet for your sakes he became poor, so that by his poverty you might become rich." If Jesus is "the way, the truth and the life," the model for our own lives and the pattern for that "life to the full" which he came to give; and if Jesus has "overcome the world," then we have nothing to fear by imitating his generosity. The gift of courage based on faith in the example and teaching of Jesus frees us from the caution which makes us cling to our possessions for security even in the face of the urgent, present need of others for physical relief or spiritual ministry.

Jesus said few words to the father of the girl he was about to raise up: "Do not fear; only believe." The Holy Spirit enriches the Church and each of her members with the gift of courage so that as a community we might live the Gospel fearlessly, in all of its length and breadth and depth and height, and minister to the needs of others with heroic freedom from the cares and anxieties of this world.

Reflecting on This Week's Gospels

Thirteenth Week of the Year

Pray daily: Lord, you felt overwhelming fear in your agony in the garden, but you overcame it out of love for the Father and for me. Give me a love for you and for others that is stronger than all fear.

Monday: Matthew 8:18-22. A scribe approached and said to him, "Teacher, I will follow you wherever you go." Do you have the courage to say this to Jesus? Have you asked for it? Where do you hold back?

Tuesday: Matthew 8:23-27. He said to them, "Why are you afraid, you of little faith?" Feelings of fear are natural. What kind of fear is a lack of faith? How should you deal with your fears?

Wednesday: Matthew 8:28-34. "The swineherds ran off, and on going to the town, they told the whole story about what had happened to the demoniacs. Then the whole town came out to meet Jesus; and when they saw him, they begged him to leave their neighborhood." Do you ever turn away from prayer or from some encounter with Jesus because you are afraid of what he might ask?

Thursday: Matthew 9:1-8. Jesus said to the paralytic, "Take heart, son; your sins are forgiven." Why does knowing you are forgiven give you the courage to rise and walk? Do you use the Sacrament of Reconciliation for this?

Friday: Matthew 9:9-13. The Pharisees said to his disciples, "Why does your teacher eat with tax collectors and sinners?" Do you ever disregard social customs or public opinion in order to reach out to others?

Saturday: Matthew 9:14-17. "Neither is new wine put into old wineskins; otherwise, the skins burst...." What do you need to change in yourself and in your life-style if you want to understand the new law of Jesus clearly enough to live it heroically?

Living This Week's Gospels

As Christian: Whenever you feel afraid, say, "Sacred Heart of Jesus, I put my trust in you, for though I fear all things from my weakness, I hope for all things from your goodness."

As Disciple: See how many you can remember (or find) of the twenty times Jesus says in the four Gospels, "Do not be afraid."

As Prophet: Each time you feel fear at the thought of saying or doing something that bears witness to Christ, ask the Holy Spirit in your heart to let you use the gift of courage.

As Priest: Give attention or respect to someone who by social custom is treated with less respect or is ignored.

As King: Write down how you are most intimidated by government, by your employers (or employees), by your social circle. Do you use intimidation at home or with others? What can you change in any of these areas?

The Gift of Piety

Ezekiel 2:2-5; 2 Corinthians 12:7-10; Mark 6:1-6

G od sent the Holy Spirit to bring to completion that "mystery" of God's loving good will toward us which was displayed in Jesus Christ; namely, in the fullness of time to gather up in Christ everything created, bringing everything in heaven and on earth into unity under Jesus as head (see Ephesians 1:8-10).

No word in human language expresses adequately this union, this relationship in Christ which is being formed to perfection by the Holy Spirit. It is love, it is communion between persons, it is the bonding that members of one family have with each other; it is more than that: It is the oneness that the members of one body have with each other through union with the head; it is being one in mind and heart and soul; it is to share in one and the same life.

And we constantly forget it. We live with a sense of dividedness, of being separate races, ethnic groups, nations, religions, political parties. We look upon every individual as separate from ourselves in varying degrees. We are jealous of one another, in competition, as if the good of one were not the good of all. We have not begun to absorb what Jesus meant when he prayed, "that they may all be one, as you, Father, are in me and I am in you."

In God there is "distinction in persons" between the Father, Son and Spirit, but "oneness in being and equality in majesty." And in the Body of Christ, which we are, we are distinct from each other as persons, but we share in one life and we are all equal in dignity and value. We are all children of the Father, heirs of heaven, members of Christ and coworkers with him, temples of the Holy Spirit. We are all brothers and sisters to each other. What benefits one should benefit all; what benefits all should benefit each individual. This is the rule of life in one body, in one family.

But we do forget it. When Jesus spoke in his hometown the people took offense. They said, "Where did this man get all this?... Is not this the carpenter, the son of Mary and brother of James and Joses and Judas and Simon? And are not his sisters here with us?" It upset them that a hometown boy should be so extraordinary. Instead of bonding with him and rejoicing, they saw him as both different from them and separate. They were threatened.

We take this attitude even toward God. We see God, not only as different, but as distant, separate from us, threatening. God, who is loyal even when we are not, has to keep taking the initiative to win us back when we rebel: "Son of man," God has said to innumerable prophets like Ezekiel, "I am sending you to the Israelites, rebels who have rebelled against me." God can never abandon us, even though a mother can abandon her child.

The virtue of loyalty to one's own—to family above all, extended to one's tribe or nation—is piety. Piety, in its real meaning, is the "gut bond" of loyalty to one's own flesh and blood. It is what holds families and societies together. Through the Holy Spirit God has given us the gift of piety, which first of all bonds us to God as Father and then extends family loyalty to every member of the human race. By this gift we say of every person on earth what Jesus said of his disciples: "Here are my mother and my brothers" (see Matthew 12:47-50).

Through piety we say with Saint Paul, "I am content with weaknesses, insults, hardships, persecutions and calamities for the sake of Christ; for whenever I am weak, then I am strong." We do not resent even humiliation or redemptive suffering, because anything which unites us more totally to Christ our head, or any suffering that benefits the whole Body of Christ on earth, is a blessing to us.

Reflecting on This Week's Gospels

Fourteenth Week of the Year

Pray daily: Lord, you chose to make the human race your own family. Give me the grace and the love to make it also my family.

Monday: Matthew 9:18-26. Jesus saw her, and said, "Take heart, daughter; your faith has made you well." Jesus was on his way to cure the synagogue leader's daughter. Why did he call this woman "daughter"? Does this say anything about his healing ministry?

Tuesday: Matthew 9:32-38. At the sight of the crowds, his heart was moved with pity for them because they were troubled and abandoned, like sheep without a shepherd. What was Jesus' attitude toward "people in general"? What is mine?

Wednesday: Matthew 10:1-7. Then he summoned his twelve disciples and gave them authority over unclean spirits to drive them out and to cure every disease and every illness. Did this mission and power give the disciples a special relationship with all people? Do you have the same mission? The same power? The same relationship?

Thursday: Matthew 10:7-15. Without cost you have received; without cost you are to give. Do you give attention and signs of friendship only to those from whom you have received friendship, or to everyone you meet?

Friday: Matthew 10:16-23. "Brother will betray brother to death, ...and children will rise against parents and have them put to death." Can you "hand over" anyone to be ridiculed or hurt by those with whom you talk without handing over brother or sister?

Saturday: Matthew 10:24-33. "[B]ut whoever denies me before others, I also will deny before my Father in heaven."

How, when, do you (in action, not words) deny the presence of Christ in others? What does Jesus have to deny about me then to the Father?

Living This Week's Gospels

As Christian: Say frequently during the day, "Lord, have mercy," conscious that to "have mercy" means to "come to the aid of another out of a sense of relationship."

As Disciple: See how many different words expressing the relationship of Jesus to us you can find in the Gospels (for example, "brother," "friend").

As Prophet: What can or would you change in your way of speaking or acting toward others if you specifically think of them as brothers or sisters?

As Priest: What do you do for relatives that you could do for all in the parish? (For example, visit or send cards to the sick, attend funerals....)

As King: What policies would you work to change in your city or where you work if the people affected by those policies were your own brothers and sisters?

Fifteenth Sunday of the Year

The Gift of Counsel

Amos 7:12-15; Ephesians 1:3-14; Mark 6:7-13

God sent the Holy Spirit to go with and guide all the members of the Church in their mission of bringing the life-giving truth and healing love of Christ to the world. Every one of us can exclaim with Amos, "I was no prophet... The LORD took me from following the flock, and said to me, 'Go, prophesy to my people.'" It is only by confidence in the Holy Spirit that we presume to take up and continue the mission of Jesus Christ on earth.

When Jesus sent his disciples out on mission he instructed them to take nothing for the journey but a walking stick—no food, no sack, no money in their belts. Their life-style was to be a visible sign that they relied, not on human resources, but on the presence and power of God. By that power they would have authority over unclean spirits, they would drive out many demons, and anoint with oil many who were sick and cure them. This same power is given to us. We are the continuance of the community Jesus founded; the Holy Spirit has been present in the Church, guiding and empowering, for almost two thousand years.

The power of the Holy Spirit does not work in the Church, or in any one of us, like magic. The Spirit truly guides us, but we have to listen. And when complex situations arise, when the right way to go is especially unclear, we have to listen with special attention. If we do not, we will not get the message. God chose to work through human beings in reality, not just in appearance. This means that the human reality of the Church, the free responses and choices of human beings, can really help, and can really hinder, the work of God. Neither miracles nor mistakes should surprise us.

The Father has truly "blessed us in Christ with every

spiritual blessing in the heavenly places." He has "made known to us the mystery of his...plan for the fullness of times." And he has "lavished on us...according to the riches of his grace." But we still have to do our part, and God's work still depends on our human decisions as well as on God's grace.

This means that we need to be in live, continuing contact with the Holy Spirit. And we need to use the "gift of the Spirit," which is an abiding, live presence of the Spirit within us. Everything is not given or settled once and for all; we need to constantly pray, ask, listen, discern and try to follow the guidance and inspiration of the Holy Spirit—every day, every week, every year. We need to do this as individuals and as a Church. All the answers are not given from the beginning, and all the directions are not set once and for all. The Spirit is alive and interactive within us. We have to be alive and interactive as well in our efforts to follow the voice of the Spirit in every choice.

To help us make right decisions, God has given us the gift of counsel. This is a gift which opens us to receive the light and guidance of the Spirit when a decision we have to make is particularly difficult because the answer is just not clear. If the answer is clear but hard to accept, we need the gift of fortitude, or courage. And for ordinary, practical decision-making on a day-to-day basis, the gift of knowledge is enough. But we need counsel when an ordinary, working knowledge of Christianity is not enough—just as, when our ordinary, working knowledge of civil law is not enough, we hire "counsel," which is another name for a lawyer.

When Jesus sent his disciples on mission he instructed them not to depend on human resources. But like a judge who instructs someone on trial to hire "counsel," Jesus instructs us not to even attempt his work without the aid of the "Paraclete"—which means "lawyer," or "advocate." A law-court proverb says, "Anyone who defends himself has a fool for a client." It is just as foolish to take on the life and mission of Jesus without making use of Counsel.

Reflecting on This Week's Gospels

Fifteenth Week of the Year

> **Pray daily:** *Lord, send forth your Spirit, and renew the face of the earth.*

Monday: Matthew 10:34 to 11:1. "I have come to set a man against his father, / and a daughter against her mother, / and a daughter-in-law against her mother-in-law...." Do you ask for counsel when you do not know whether your stand on the Gospel is too rigid or too compromising?

Tuesday: Matthew 11:20-24. "Woe to you, Bethsaida! For if the deeds of power done in you had been done in Tyre and Sidon, they would have repented long ago in sackcloth and ashes." Do you ever worry about missing inspirations from the Holy Spirit inviting you to aim at something better or higher?

Wednesday: Matthew 11:25-27. "I thank you, Father, Lord of heaven and earth, because you have hidden these things from the wise and the intelligent and have revealed them to infants." Do you ever excuse yourself from taking a stand about religious issues because you are not professionally trained in theology?

Thursday: Matthew 11:28-30. "Take my yoke upon you, and learn from me; for I am gentle and humble in heart, and you will find rest for your souls." When you do not feel at peace, do you ask for guidance from the Holy Spirit, the Consoler?

Friday: Matthew 12:1-8. "If you knew what this meant, 'I desire mercy, not sacrifice,' you would not have condemned the guiltless." Do you look for the reason behind each of God's laws (or Church laws) and try to follow the true spirit behind each one rather than the letter?

Saturday: Matthew 12:14-21. "But the Pharisees went out and conspired against him, how to destroy him." How often, when you take counsel with others, do you feel that the Holy Spirit is present? Do we sometimes decide to "destroy" someone rather than to save that person through love?

Living This Week's Gospels

As Christian: Develop the habit of praying before every decision you make, giving to it whatever time is possible or appropriate.

As Disciple: Try to match a Scripture text to each of the significant characteristics of your life-style.

As Prophet: Identify one decision that you did not make or do not think you can make just on reason and religious principles alone without the help of the Holy Spirit's counsel.

As Priest: Ask counsel from the Holy Spirit in order to deal in a life-giving way with some particular person in your life.

As King: With the help of the Spirit's counsel, look for a practical way to change one thing in your environment (at home, at work, in your social life) that clashes with the reign of God.

The Gift of Knowledge

Jeremiah 23:1-6; Ephesians 2:13-18; Mark 6:30-34

God sent the Holy Spirit to guide the Church and each of her members along the practical path to life in its fullness. God's intent is not just that we should know but that we should grow—grow in understanding by the gift of understanding; grow in appreciation of the things of God by the gift of wisdom; grow in response to God by free acts of the will supported by the gifts of awe, piety and courage. To guide us in our choices the Holy Spirit enlightens us with the gifts of counsel and of knowledge.

Knowledge is the gift of practical know-how in the spiritual life. It shows us how to use everything for spiritual growth, how things fit into the practical picture: prayer, woundedness, relationships, temptations, inspirations, sacraments, all the multiple elements which are the "daily bread" of our human and graced existence. We use the gift of counsel in particularly complex situations, when we need special help from the Holy Spirit to know what we should do. But we use knowledge for the practical, everyday management of our spiritual lives.

Jeremiah preaches "woe to the shepherds who destroy and scatter the sheep" of God's pasture. This applies, not just to pastors, but to every person who does—or could—influence others in any group situation, including family and social life, business and politics. It also applies to the way we manage our own lives. Before anything else, we are shepherds of our own souls. God has entrusted us to ourselves, that we might nourish ourselves with everything that will help us grow in grace. We will answer to God's love for our stewardship.

We see in Jesus the model of the good shepherd who leads and governs wisely. To his disciples, tired from the efforts of their first missionary tour, he says, "Come away and rest a while." He constantly says this to us: "Come. Take a break. Let me talk to you, let me teach you. Come especially when you feel you are so heavily burdened that you do not have time to stop—and you will find rest for your souls."

When Jesus sees us being lured away from his pastures by the enticements and pressures of this world, by all of our secondary goals and preoccupations, he has compassion for us, because we are "like sheep without a shepherd." Then he invites us to come aside and let him "teach us many things."

Our biggest failure as believers in Jesus is not malice; it is bad management of our lives. We do not make use of what God makes available to us: Scripture, sacraments, liturgy, private prayer, the gifts of the Holy Spirit. We forget our priorities, putting last things first and leaving first things to last. We give "prime time" to the voices of the culture and little or no time to the voice of God. None of this is malice; it is just bad management. But it is our fault.

How does Jesus teach us? He does it from "outside" through parents, teachers, pastors and laity who minister to us; through friends who share with us their experience of responding to God in faith; through those who write books and give talks, through any person or event which gives us insight into the process of interaction with God. And he does it from "inside" by the gift of the Holy Spirit enlightening our minds as we read, listen and pray, giving us appreciation for the things of God. The gift of knowledge lets us recognize what is available and shows us what we need to do in order to let Jesus teach us and lead us to life in its fullness. But we must choose to act on the knowledge.

This gift is especially active when we use the Sacrament of Reconciliation as a periodic review of our performance as managers of our lives. Reconciliation helps us see how everything fits together in our lives, what is missing and what our next step should be.

Reflecting on This Week's Gospels

Sixteenth Week of the Year

Pray daily: Lord, we are your sheep; you are our shepherd. Teach us. And show me how to come to you and learn.

Monday: Matthew 12:38-42. "The people of Nineveh will rise up at the judgment with this generation and condemn it, because they repented at the proclamation of Jonah, and see, something greater than Jonah is here!" How many things do you have to help you grow spiritually that the Ninevites did not have? How do you use them?

Tuesday: Matthew 12:46-50. "For whoever does the will of my Father in heaven is my brother and sister and mother." What practical help do you draw from knowing Jesus loves you and relates to you this way?

Wednesday: Matthew 13:1-9. And he told them many things in parables, saying: "Listen! A sower went out to sow.... Let anyone with ears listen." This parable says three things block the growth of grace in us—what are they? How can you use this knowledge?

Thursday: Matthew 13:10-17. "[T]o those who have, more will be given, and they will have an abundance; but from those who have nothing, even what they have will be taken away." What are your spiritual riches? How do you spend them?

Friday: Matthew 13:18-23. "But as for what was sown on good soil, this is the one who hears the word and understands it, who indeed bears fruit and yields, in one case a hundredfold, in another sixty, and in another thirty." When you hear God's word, do you think about it in terms of how you might put it into practice?

Saturday: Matthew 13:24-30. The householder replied, "No; for in gathering the weeds you would uproot the wheat along with them." How can stamping out evil in someone, or in the Church, also stamp out good?

Living This Week's Gospels

As Christian: Put your knowledge of Jesus as Savior to work by praying to him every day this week for one special need.

As Disciple: Put your knowledge of Jesus as Teacher to work by reading and reflecting on one passage of Scripture each day this week.

As Prophet: Put your knowledge of the Spirit's presence within you to work by asking him to show you one thing in your life-style you can change in order to bear clearer witness to Christ. Then think.

As Priest: Put your awareness of sharing in the priesthood of Jesus to work by consciously trying as the Body of Christ to heal someone's woundedness.

As King: Put your knowledge of Christ's victory over sin and death to work by overcoming your fear and trying to change something around you which you know needs to be changed.

Spirit of Focus

2 Kings 4:42-44; Ephesians 4:1-6; John 6:1-15

A community is a "common unity," not only of commitment, but of appreciation. A true community is made up of people who value the same things, who have the same essential priorities.

When Jesus multiplied the bread and fish to feed the crowd that followed him, their reaction showed that they were not ready to be the kind of community he had come to form. It was because he showed he could give them bread, prosperity, that they acclaimed him the messiah they were waiting for. Jesus saw that they just wanted him to be their king, to see that they enjoyed the good things of this world. That was when he realized they were not really with him. He "withdrew again to the mountain alone," not just to escape them, but because he realized how deeply alone he already was.

When the Church assembles for the Eucharistic liturgy, it is so that Jesus might do what he previewed in this miracle. When John wrote in his Gospel that "Jesus took the loaves, and when he had given thanks, he distributed them...." he was deliberately echoing the words the early Christians were familiar with from the liturgy: Jesus "took bread, said the blessing, broke the bread, and gave it to his disciples saying, "Take and eat it: this is my Body" *(Sacramentary,* page 558). Christians come to church not to increase their chances of living a secure and painless life in this world, but to seek what Jesus came to give: union of mind and heart and will with God, union with Jesus himself in one shared, divine life of grace, in one shared, divine mission of saving the world. They come for communion: communion with God in Christ, communion with each other in the Holy Spirit, communion with Jesus by taking in the gift of his Body and Blood in Holy Communion.

This is what makes the Church a community: the "common union" of appreciation all have for what the religion of Jesus is all about. The presider's greeting at Mass expresses it: "The grace of our Lord Jesus Christ, the love of God, and the communion of the Holy Spirit be with you all" (see 2 Corinthians 13:13). From the very beginning of our celebration it is clear what we are seeking, what we have assembled for. It is not for entertainment or a "meaningful liturgy" which will leave us on a spiritual high; not for "togetherness"; not for social reform or any project which will give us a sense of contributing to the human race; not for the sake of programs which will give us emotional healing or help us to raise our children; and it is not to keep God on our side in our various enterprises. We do not assemble because we hope God will make us healthy or wealthy, but because he has already made us wise.

Wisdom is the gift of the Holy Spirit which gives us appreciation for spiritual things: for God and the spiritual gifts of God. The Latin word for wisdom, *sapientia,* comes from the word for taste: *sapor,* "savor." Wisdom gives us a "taste" for spiritual things. It is the gift best associated with Eucharist, when God invites us to receive the bread of life, to "taste and see that the Lord is good."

What makes us able to assemble authentically as the community Jesus founded is our "common unity" in appreciating the kind of messiah, of Savior, Jesus really came to be. Because we have, by the gift of the Spirit, the wisdom to value his spiritual gifts above all else, we are able to share our own gifts of faith, hope and love with each other and to support each other by expressing that "unity of the Spirit" which lets us experience ourselves as "one body and one Spirit called to the one hope" that is the foundation and goal of our lives.

Reflecting on This Week's Gospels

Seventeenth Week of the Year

Pray daily: Lord, through the gift of your Body and Blood, increase my desire for union with you in everything I do.

Monday: Matthew 13:31-35. "Jesus told the crowds all these things in parables; without a parable he told them nothing." Do spiritual things like Mass, retreats, adult religious education courses, parish missions, Bible study and frequent use of Reconciliation mean something to you? Why is this?

Tuesday: Matthew 13:36-43. Jesus said in reply, "[T]he field is the world, the good seed are the children of the kingdom; the weeds are the children of the evil one, and the enemy who sowed them is the devil." How many of your values and priorities come consciously from the gospel? How many from the culture?

Wednesday: Matthew 13:44-46. "[T]he kingdom of heaven is like a merchant in search of fine pearls; on finding one pearl of great value, he went and sold all that he had and bought it." What have you made sacrifices to attain? Are these primarily spiritual values or values only of this world?

Thursday: Matthew 13:47-53. "[T]he kingdom of heaven is like a net that was thrown into the sea and caught fish of every kind; when it is full, they drew it ashore, sat down, and put the good into baskets but threw out the bad." Where do the good and bad priorities in your life come from? Does tracing their origin help you decide which are good, which are bad?

Friday: Matthew 13:54-58. "Jesus said to them, 'Prophets are not without honor except in their own country and in their own house.' And he did not do many deeds of power there, because of their unbelief." How often has not wanting to hear something, or not wanting to hear it from a particular person, blocked you from seeing the truth?

Saturday: Matthew 14:1-12. Salome said, "'Give me the head of John the Baptist here on a platter.' The king [Herod] was grieved, yet out of regard for his oaths and for his guests, he commanded it to be given." What values or beliefs of your own have you denied to please people?

Living This Week's Gospels

As Christian: Notice what things the Church asks for in the Mass prayers. What are her priorities?

As Disciple: Study the Introductory Rites of the Mass (from the Sign of the Cross through Opening Prayer), asking what values are proclaimed.

As Prophet: This week sacrifice one value of this world (for example, what you spend time, money, energy on) for some spiritual value.

As Priest: Share your "loaves and fishes" with someone by giving expression to your spiritual values and priorities.

As King: Ask what values are affirmed by the people with whom you work, live or recreate. Do something to promote awareness of spiritual or human values over material or cultural ones.

Eighteenth Sunday of the Year

Spirit of Discipleship

Exodus 16:2-4, 12-15; Ephesians 4:17, 20-24; John 6:24-35

The Introductory Rites of the Mass announce us as a community assembled in appreciation of values not of this world: the grace of our Lord Jesus Christ, the love of God and communion in the Holy Spirit. The Liturgy of the Word builds this appreciation by teaching us what it means to share in the divine life and mission of Jesus by grace; what the love of God for us has been throughout history and what it is today. Through the Scripture readings, homily, Profession of Faith and Intercessory Prayers, this part of the Mass forms us to that "common unity" of mind and heart which is communion in the Holy Spirit.

Our first reaction to all this might sometimes be the same as that of the Israelites when God fed them with manna from heaven: "What is it?" they asked each other, "For they did not know what it was." They were used to the meat and bread they ate as slaves in the land of Egypt. Moses had to explain to them, "It is the bread that the LORD has given you to eat."

Jesus explains that it was not Moses who gave us the true bread from heaven, but the Father gives it in sending Jesus: "For the bread of God is that which comes down from heaven and gives life to the world." And Jesus tells us, "Do not work for the food that perishes, but for the food that endures for eternal life."

This bread is first of all the word of God. It comes down from heaven from God who alerted us, "[M]y thoughts are not your thoughts, / nor are your ways my ways.... / For as the heavens are higher than the earth,/ so are my ways higher than your ways / and my thoughts than your thoughts." So naturally we find ourselves saying in response to his words, "What is this?" We are used to the attitudes and values we are constantly being fed by our culture, within which we are just as enslaved as the Jews were in Egypt. We do not recognize at first the "bread from heaven" as fulfilling. That is why Jesus insists on faith in the power of his words to lead us to true satisfaction: "I am the bread of life. Whoever comes to me will never be hungry, and whoever believes in me will never be thirsty." He is teaching us wisdom—appreciation for what is spiritual, for God and the things of God.

Paradoxically, our instinct for survival is most concerned about that part of us which cannot possibly survive: the body. We hunger most consciously for the perishable food which can only nourish what is perishable. Jesus urges us to work for the imperishable food which nourishes eternal life in us. And the work which gains us this food is simply believing: "This is the work of God, that you believe in him whom he has sent."

Believing does not mean just sitting around feeling convinced. Every act of belief (and every real human judgment, for that matter) is a free choice, a free decision to affirm that something is true. The work of believing in Jesus is discipleship: deliberately choosing by faith to read and reflect on Jesus' words and to use them as our guidance system; deliberately basing our choice of goals and objectives on hope in his promises; deliberately choosing to respond with love to every person, in every word and action, at every moment of our lives.

Once we have "learned Christ" and received from him the gift of Wisdom through the Holy Spirit poured out in our hearts, we must "no longer live as the Gentiles do, in the futility of their minds," but rather "put away our former way of life, our old self, corrupt and deluded by its lusts, and to be renewed in the spirit of our minds, and to clothe ourselves with the new self, created according to the likeness of God in true righteousness and holiness."

This is the way of wisdom proclaimed and nourished in the Eucharistic celebration.

Reflecting on This Week's Gospels

Eighteenth Week of the Year

Pray daily: Lord, increase my faith in your words as the true bread that nourishes life in me. Draw me to seek you in word and sacrament.

Monday: Matthew 14:13-21. Jesus said the blessing, broke the loaves, and gave them to the disciples, who in turn gave them to the crowds. They all ate and were satisfied. What does Jesus offer you to nourish your soul? When? Do you eat? are you satisfied?

Tuesday: Matthew 14:22-36. After they got into the boat, the wind died down. Those who were in the boat did him homage, saying, "Truly, you are the Son of God." What events in your life have made you appreciate more who Jesus really is?

Wednesday: Matthew 15:21-28. She said, "Lord, yet even the dogs eat the crumbs that fall from their masters' table." Then Jesus said to her in reply, "Woman, great is your faith! Let it be done for you as you wish." Do you really appreciate the words of God available to you in Scripture? How do you show it? With what result?

Thursday: Matthew 16:13-23. Jesus asked his disciples, "Who do people say that the Son of Man is?... But who do you say that I am?" When, how did you discover Jesus personally, as contrasted with just learning about him from others?

Friday: Matthew 16:24-28. "For what will it profit them if they gain the whole world but forfeit their life? Or what will they give in return for their life?" Are you more focused on enhancing your human life in this world or on enhancing your divine life?

Saturday: Matthew 17:14-20. "For truly I tell you, if you have faith the size of a mustard seed, you will say to this mountain, 'Move from here to there,' and it will move; and nothing will be impossible for you." How does the Eucharistic celebration increase your faith? How could you make it help you more?

Living This Week's Gospels

As Christian: "Enthrone" (make a place of honor for) the Bible in your room or home to show its place in your life.

As Disciple: Take one of the Eucharistic Prayers and see how many themes from Scripture you can identify in it.

As Prophet: Look at the books and periodicals in your house. What does this selection say about your interests and values?

As Priest: Offer one person the "bread of life" this week by giving a book, a magazine subscription, an invitation to something that nourishes spiritual values.

As King: Ask what policies or practices in your family, professional or social life seem inconsistent with the words you say or hear during the Eucharistic celebration. Is there anything you can change?

Nineteenth Sunday of the Year

Spirit of Cooperation

1 Kings 19:4-8; Ephesians 4:30-5:2; John 6:41-51

Wisdom is the gift that gives appreciation for spiritual, divine things. It is nourished by Eucharist. But one part of the Eucharistic celebration proclaims in a special way the value of what is created and human. And surprisingly this, too, is wisdom. To see the ability of the human to be made divine is to appreciate the divine value of what is human.

The basic principle for understanding Jesus is "fully human, fully divine." And this gives us the basic rule for understanding the Church, our own reality as people who share in the life of God by grace, and for evaluating Christian behavior. In everything we see or say about ourselves or the Church, and in every judgment we make about the way we should act as Christians, we must be careful to fully accept and fully respect what is human in us and what is divine.

The prayer during the preparation of the gifts of bread and wine (Offertory) during Mass expresses strikingly our belief in the value of all that is created, of everything human: "God of all creation... this bread... which earth has given and human hands have made... this wine, fruit of the vine and work of human hands...." We believe that these created things, produced by human labor, can actually become for us "spiritual drink" and "bread of [divine] life," and that we can "share in the divinity of Christ" who took flesh to "share in our humanity."

Jesus' own people could not believe that someone so human could be divine: "Is this not Jesus, the son of Joseph, whose father and mother we know? How can he now say, 'I have come down from heaven'?" The sinfulness of the clergy and hierarchy in the sixteenth century led many Christians to take the protesting (or "protestant") stance that God could not endow flawed human beings with the divine power we associate with priestly ministry or the teaching authority of pope and bishops. The protestant rejection of the Church was actually a rejection of human nature's capacity to be the instrument of divine action by grace. Whatever affirmed the value of human beings as real cooperators with God in the work of redemption was looked on with suspicion. The first victim was the Church herself, and then the sacraments (especially Eucharist and Reconciliation) and veneration of human saints, especially Mary, the human mother of God.

All of us get discouraged at times with human nature in general and our own in particular. We feel like Elijah: "It is enough; now, O LORD, take away my life, for I am no better than my ancestors." But to give in to this discouragement would be to "grieve the Holy Spirit of God, with which you were marked with a seal for the day of redemption." Saint Paul urges us instead to believe that we can "be imitators of God, as beloved children, and live in love, as Christ loved us."

We do not just believe this; we express our belief by an action, a choice, which would not make sense without it. Believing that Baptism has made us truly one with Jesus who "handed himself over for us as a sacrificial offering to God," we offer ourselves to God together with him to be used to give divine life to others. In Christ and with Christ we "offer our bodies as a living sacrifice to God," our "flesh for the life of the world." We commit ourselves to giving flesh to his words in life-giving acts of witness.

This is the Catholic "altar call." At the Presentation of Gifts we place bread and wine on the altar as symbols of ourselves. During the readings we offered our minds to be transformed by God's word. Now, as we offer the bread and wine to be transformed into the Body and Blood of Christ, we offer ourselves to be so transformed into the perfect likeness of Christ, whose body we became at Baptism, that everything we say and do will bear witness to the Gospel. To appreciate in faith the value of this offering is to experience the gift of wisdom.

Reflecting on This Week's Gospels

Nineteenth Week of the Year

Pray daily: Lord, as many grains of wheat are ground together, mixed with water and baked with fire to become one bread, we ask you to form your Church by the water of Baptism and the fire of the Holy Spirit, that we might give life to the world.

Monday: Matthew 17:22-27. "You will find [in its mouth] a coin; take that and give it to them for you and for me." In how many ways has Jesus associated himself with you? How does the Offertory express your association with him in his mission?

Tuesday: Matthew 18:1-5,10,12-14. "Whoever becomes humble like this child is the greatest in the kingdom of heaven." How does the offering of yourself with the bread and wine make you like a child?

Wednesday: Matthew 18:15-20. "Again, truly I tell you, if two of you agree on earth about anything you ask, it will be done for you by my Father in heaven. For where two or three are gathered in my name, I am there among them." How do the bread and wine express our unity with each other? What do you think about when they are presented at the Offertory?

Thursday: Matthew 18:21-19:1. "I forgave you all that debt because you pleaded with me. Should you not have had mercy on your fellow slave, as I had mercy on you?" How at the Offertory do we show mercy to others as God has to us?

Friday: Matthew 19:3-12. "[W]hat God has joined together, let no one separate." How do bread and wine symbolize the way God has joined us to each other in the Church?

Saturday: Matthew 19:13-15. "Then little children were being brought to him in order that he might lay his hands on them and pray." How and how often do you explicitly bring children (or adult children of God) to Jesus? Do you present them as the bread and wine? For what?

Living This Week's Gospels

As Christian: At the Offertory of the Mass, consciously offer yourself to be transformed into the perfect image of Christ, to find all your fulfillment in being his Body on earth.

As Disciple: During the readings at Mass, offer your mind—all your attitudes and values—to be transformed by God's word.

As Prophet: At the Offertory of the Mass, offer your body as a "living sacrifice to God" to bear witness to the truth and values of Christ in every word, choice and action. (Read Romans 12:1-2.)

As Priest: At the Offertory, explicitly "die" to being a single grain of wheat in order to be one bread with others in a community of shared life, ministry and mission.

As King: At the Offertory of the Mass, offer your flesh for the life of the world, asking God to use you to bring about changes in your environment: in your family, social, professional and civic life.

Twentieth Sunday of the Year

Spirit of Stewardship

Proverbs 9:1-6; Ephesians 5:15-20; John 6:51-58

Receiving the Body and Blood of Christ in Communion is probably the fastest and easiest way to grow in wisdom—that is, in appreciation for God and the things of God. At the Communion Service of the Mass we can hear the prophet calling, "[Wisdom] has also set her table. / '...Come, eat of my bread, / and drink of the wine I have mixed. / Lay aside immaturity, and live, / and walk in the way of insight.'"

Jesus said it even more emphatically and in explicit detail: "Those who eat my flesh and drink my blood...abide in me and I in them"; "have eternal life"; and Jesus "will raise them on the last day."

To know the meaning of these words is understanding. To appreciate them is wisdom.

Why is it that some people seem drawn to deeper union with God while others do not? Why do some people just have a taste for prayer, for learning about God, for deepening their understanding of Scripture, for using the Sacrament of Reconciliation, for taking part in the Eucharistic celebration, for making retreats, for sharing in the redemptive mission of Christ through ministry and explicitly apostolic acts? Why does religion seem to take first place with some people and not with others?

Too easy is the answer Karl Marx gave: "Religion is the opium of the people." It is true that many people come to God out of need, seeking relief from emotional distress, asking to be delivered from pain, fear or loneliness. It is even more true that those who do not recognize their need to find ultimate relief from these things in God are living in deluded superficiality. "Blessed are the poor in spirit (those who recognize their own inadequacy), for theirs is the kingdom of God." Woe to those who feel they have it made; they are not open to God.

The question remains, however: Why is it that some people appreciate the value of deeper relationship with God as the way to the fullness of life, while for others—believing, practicing, churchgoing Christians—religion is important but not primary; a part of their life but not their very life? To state the question theologically, why do some people seem to have the gift of wisdom while others do not?

No single, simple answer is adequate, of course, but we have our Lord's words: "Unless you eat the flesh of the Son of Man and drink his blood, you have no life in you." Communion is a way to "taste and see that the LORD is good." The more we experience union with God in the Eucharist, the more we desire to grow into deeper union with God, and the more religion becomes for us our life, which is the only valid way to understand or practice it.

Appreciation for life is the key to appreciation of religion. If we are willing to settle for less, religion will not be important to us. We can observe all the rules and practices of our religion in a minimal way, even doing a little more than what is explicitly required, and never experience that life to the full Jesus came to give. But if we desire to know truth in its fullness, to know Jesus intimately, to enter into relationship with others on the deepest level of each one's core response to God, to experience love in which we lose and find ourselves in total surrender and possession, to probe the length and breadth and height and depth of our own being, our capacity to know, to love and to live—and if we want life that gets better and better forever: graced life, eternal life, divine life—then we can appreciate the religion which the first Christians called simply "this new way," the way to live life to the full. It is only from this perspective of appreciating life in its fullness that we can take responsibility, as stewards of the kingship of Christ, for the life and the world entrusted to us.

Reflecting on This Week's Gospels

Twentieth Week of the Year

> *Pray daily: Lord, to us, your Church, you have
> entrusted the treasure of your Body and Blood.
> Fill me with desire to make this gift available
> to the whole world.*

Monday: Matthew 19:16-22. The young man said to Jesus,
"I have kept all these [commandments]; what do I still lack?"
Jesus said to him, "If you wish to be perfect, go, sell your
possessions and give the money to the poor, and you will
have treasure in heaven; then come, follow me." What desire
do you feel to grow in intimacy with God? Is just keeping
the commandments enough to satisfy you? Why?

Tuesday: Matthew 19:23-30. "[I]t is easier for a camel to
go through the eye of a needle than for one who is rich to
enter the kingdom of God." How do your own riches
(material or other) affect your desire for God?

Wednesday: Matthew 20:1-16. "[T]he kingdom of heaven
is like a landowner who went out early in the morning to hire
laborers for his vineyard." What relationship with Christ does
receiving Communion express? Have you taken responsibility
for his vineyard?

Thursday: Matthew 22:1-14. "The kingdom of heaven
may be compared to a king who gave a wedding banquet for
his son." In how many different ways is Communion like a
wedding feast? How often are you invited? What is
your response?

Friday: Matthew 22:34-40. "You shall love the Lord, your
God, with all your heart and with all your soul, and with all
your mind. This is the greatest and first commandment."
Which is the greatest of all the sacraments? Why?

Saturday: Matthew 23:1-12: "The greatest among you will
be your servant. All who exalt themselves will be humbled,

and all who humble themselves will be exalted." What relationship with others does receiving Communion express? Why?

Living This Week's Gospels

As Christian: Prepare for Communion by thinking about Christ's words, "Those who eat my flesh will live forever."

As Disciple: Examine the Communion Service of the Mass to see what theme-word occurs most frequently.

As Prophet: At Communion examine how you, as Christ's Body, can use your sight, hearing, speech, taste, touch as Jesus used his.

As Priest: Consecrate yourself at Communion to speak and act in a way that will promote peace and unity between all the people you deal with.

As King: Examine the possibility of bringing Communion to someone sick or homebound.

Twenty-First Sunday of the Year

Spirit of Identification

Joshua 24:1-2, 15-17, 18; Ephesians 5:21-30; John 6:60-69

A ppreciation for life is the only thing that lets us appreciate death. Only the life Jesus promises— everlasting life, divine life—makes death desirable or even acceptable. But appreciation of death as the entrance into eternal life depends on a faith that is not easy to maintain. In fact, our attitude toward death is the ultimate test of our belief in that "life to the full" which Jesus won for us on the cross.

When Jesus said, "The bread that I will give for the life of the world is my flesh" and "Those who eat my flesh and drink my blood have eternal life," many of his disciples found this a "hard saying" and broke with him.

What shocked them was not just the words "eat my flesh." This Gospel was written for the early Christian community who knew Jesus was talking about Eucharist. What they found hard to believe was the whole mystery of Christ as the Son of God who came down from heaven, took flesh, died on the cross, and now gives eternal life to all who believe and are made one with him through the grace given in word and sacrament. The hard saying is everything we celebrate in the Mass.

When Peter expresses the faith of all in response to Jesus' question, "Do you also wish to go away?" this matches the passages in Matthew, Mark and Luke where Peter's confession of faith is followed by Jesus' announcement that he is going to save the world by dying. This too is a hard saying—in reality, the same hard saying, because Eucharist is inseparable from the mystery of Christ's redemptive death. As Paul wrote to the Corinthians, "For as often as you eat this bread and drink the cup, you proclaim the Lord's death until he comes." What we celebrate in Eucharist is the value of Christ's death, which gives us a totally different attitude toward death and an entirely new appreciation of life. And this appreciation is "the wisdom of the cross."

We are invited to express our belief during the Eucharistic celebration when the Body and Blood of Christ are lifted up before the eyes of the congregation as Jesus was "lifted up" on the cross. This moment (we call it the Consecration/Elevation) follows the "institution narrative," in which the Church tells again the story of how Jesus instituted the Eucharist: He "took bread, blessed and broke it, and gave it to his disciples, saying, 'Take this, all of you, and eat it: This is my body, which will be given up for you.'" It is an invitation to all who are present to join Jesus in offering ourselves to the Father and for the human race: "our flesh for the life of the world."

The reason why we are able to offer ourselves with Jesus during the Mass is that we were, in fact, offered with and in him on the cross. The body that hung on the cross was the Body of Christ, head and members. In his crucifixion Jesus took into his own body all of those who would be "baptized into his death" until the end of the world and he let his body be put to death to take away the sins of the world. The Mass does not repeat this moment of Christ's death, but makes it present so that we who are his Body on earth today can consciously offer ourselves with and in Christ as "victims in the Victim" to take away the sins of the world. We do this as Jesus did, by responding to evil with love, by enduring whatever injustice and oppression is inflicted on us and loving back—which includes trying to stop injustice by every means compatible with love.

Every Eucharist challenges us to decide today whose wisdom we will follow: that of this world, which "God has made foolish," or that of "Christ crucified," which is foolishness by the light of every human society. If Christ, then we offer ourselves with him in every Eucharist to serve others in love: our flesh for the life of the world.

Reflecting on This Week's Gospels

Twenty-First Week of the Year

> *Pray daily: Lord, I give you my body that in me you might continue to save the world through love. Convert me from violence to your way of peace.*

Monday: Matthew 23:13-22. "You blind ones, which is greater, the gift, or the altar that makes the gift sacred?" Which is greater, your human life, or your life offered with Christ on the altar for the life of the world?

Tuesday: Matthew 23:23-26. "[B]lind Pharisee! First clean the inside of the cup, so that the outside also may become clean." Have you made a deep, interior decision to live offered for others in love in union with Christ?

Wednesday: Matthew 23:27-32: "[A]nd you say, 'If we had lived in the days of our ancestors, we would not have taken part with them in shedding the blood of the prophets.'" If you had lived in the time of slavery, would you have owned slaves? Would you have accepted racial segregation? What is done by good Christians in your day that you do not accept?

Thursday: Matthew 24:42-51. "Therefore, you also must be ready, for the Son of Man is coming at an unexpected hour." Do you recognize Jesus coming to you when things go wrong as well as when they go right? When is it easier to recognize him?

Friday: Matthew 25:1-13. "The foolish [bridesmaids] took their lamps, they took no oil with them; but the wise took flasks of oil with their lamps." In your experience, what is the "oil" which best feeds the flame of faith and love in you?

Saturday: Matthew 25:14-30. "His master said to him, 'Well done, good and trustworthy slave; you have been trustworthy in a few things, I will put you in charge of many things; enter into the joy of your master.'" In how many

small, easy ways can you offer yourself with Christ for the
life of the world?

Living This Week's Gospels

As Christian: Renounce all use of violence as an act
of faith and trust in Jesus as Savior.

As Disciple: Read and compare John 6:41-71 and
Matthew 16:1-28. What facts, ideas or images do
they have in common?

As Prophet: Think of a nonviolent way to handle some
situation you normally would handle with violent words
(shouting, cursing) or actions (angry gestures, slamming
doors, sulking, retaliation).

As Priest: Whenever someone offends you, think of how
Jesus looks on that person, the woundedness he sees, the
desire he has to heal. Then be merciful.

As King: In two columns list the violent and nonviolent
ways situations are handled where you work (or at home,
or in your city). Is there any one of the violent ways you
could begin to change?

Twenty-Second Sunday of the Year

Why Be a Disciple?

Deuteronomy 4:1-2, 6-8; James 1:17-18, 21-22, 27;
Mark 7:1-8, 14-15, 21-23

T he problem with the Pharisees was that they
concentrated on keeping rules instead of on learning.
Their focus was on morality instead of on discipleship.
We make the same mistake.

To focus on morality is to presume that we already
know everything we have to do, and that now we just have
to do it. To presume this is not to give much credit to Jesus
as Teacher! It is to assume that all Jesus has to teach us can
be learned in a few years of religious instruction—that it can
all be reduced to a set of simple rules. It is to presume that
we already have the mind and heart of Christ: that we think,
desire and judge authentically like him in all the complex
situations of our lives.

When Jesus blames the Pharisees for leaving aside
God's commandments to focus instead on human tradition,
he is criticizing a mistake we still make—a mistake it is
most natural to make. Teachers always tend to go to the
source themselves, interpret it, simplify it, then teach their
interpretation to their students. Once the teacher has reduced
some great principle to a few cut-and-dried rules of conduct,
the students will probably never learn more than these.
The genius of a good teacher is to reduce complexity to
simplicity. But this can also be the teacher's greatest sin—
especially when what the teacher is making simple is the
infinite truth of God!

Our teachers did this to us. They may not have had
any other choice when we were children: Can children deal
with great general principles that require deep thought and
insightful application to changing circumstances? I flunked

math in college because I did what I was taught to do in high school: I "did my homework." It was too late when my old high school teacher explained to me that what I really should have done was work enough math problems to really understand what the professor was teaching. I did only what I was told to do. But I needed more. That is why I flunked.

How many children have been taught, "If you study hard in school, you will be a success in life"—only to learn later that being a success has very little to do with earning money, and that a good education does not even guarantee you will be able to do that? But we keep things simple for children.

We teach children that to be pure means to avoid certain particular actions that are impure. But we do not teach them what real purity of heart is or how to cultivate it.

An unavoidable example we must face in our day is the commandment, "You shall not kill." We teach children very simply that it is allowed to execute criminals and to kill enemies in war. We do not teach them that this is not to be found anywhere in the teaching of Jesus and cannot be based on anything Jesus said. Our traditional teaching about capital punishment and war is simply an interpretation—a human tradition—which developed over the ages and which the Church has never condemned. Like slavery and racial segregation, the killing of enemies is something which at first glance is obviously contrary to the gospel, but which teachers in the Church have interpreted as justifiable under certain circumstances. Is it justifiable? The Church has not given a final answer to that. This leaves each of us with the choice of continuing to accept the human tradition we were taught as children or of looking deeply at the teaching of Jesus ourselves in order to come to our own position as adults. This does not mean we will reject anything the Church teaches as the law of Jesus; just that we look at what the Church does not teach as his law—but just as human interpretation—and reconsider that.

To look at the teaching of Jesus ourselves as it is found in the Gospel, and not as it has been given to us pre-chewed and pre-digested by our teachers, is what it means to become disciples. Until we begin to do this we are still "infants" in the faith (see 1 Corinthians 3:1).

Reflecting on This Week's Gospels

Twenty-Second Week of the Year

> *Pray daily: Lord, give me the grace to believe in you as the Teacher of life. Give me desire to live life to the full, and not to lose out on any of the experience you offer me. Teach me to take you seriously and to learn from you.*

Monday: Luke 4:16-30. "The Spirit of the Lord is upon me,/ because he has anointed me / to bring good news to the poor. / He has sent me to proclaim release to the captives / and recovery of sight to the blind, / to let the oppressed go free...." Can these great promises be fulfilled by people who just focus on keeping rules? What more do you do?

Tuesday: Luke 4:31-37. They were all amazed and said to one another, "What kind of utterance is this? For with authority and power he commands the unclean spirits, and out they come!" What is the greatest power in your words? Brilliance? Authority? Or is it love?

Wednesday: Luke 4:38-44. Jesus said to them, "I must proclaim the good news of the kingdom of God to the other cities also; for I was sent for this purpose." What do you look for most from Jesus: healing or teaching? A higher standard of living or higher standards in living?

Thursday: Luke 5:1-11. After Jesus had finished speaking, he said to Simon, "Put out into the deep water and let down your nets for a catch." Are you willing to "put out into deep water" with Jesus for the same purpose? What would it mean for you to do this?

Friday: Luke 5:33-39. "[N]ew wine must be put into fresh wineskins." What basic change has to take place in our every goal in life before we can really hear Christ's words?

Saturday: Luke 6:1-5. Then Jesus said to them, "The Son of Man is lord of the Sabbath." Is Jesus truly Lord of everything in your life? How does this show in your words and actions?

Living This Week's Gospels

As Christian: Write down, "I believe that Jesus is the Way. Therefore..."; "I believe that Jesus is the Truth. Therefore..."; "I believe that Jesus is the Life. Therefore...". Then complete the sentences.

As Disciple: Each day this week take one saying of Jesus seriously and reflect on it. Use the daily readings above if you like.

As Prophet: Picture to yourself where the telephone book is in your house, then where the Bible is. If what you see tells you that you do not rely on the Bible as much as the telephone book, change something.

As Priest: Each morning take to work (or school, or shopping, or wherever you meet people) something from the Scriptures to share with others, just as in some offices people bring snacks. Do not be obnoxious in the way you share it; just look for acceptable ways.

As King: Ask what needs to be changed in your home— physically or otherwise—in order to give Christ more room there.

Twenty-Third Sunday of the Year

Believing Is Seeing

Isaiah 35:4-7; James 2:1-5; Mark 7:31-37

Ephphatha is a word Jesus actually spoke to each one of us—and it had more effect then than it did on the deaf man in the Gospel. During our Baptism, Jesus, acting in and through the minister, touched our ears with his hand and spoke to us the word, *ephphatha,* which means, "Be opened," praying that our ears might be opened to hear the words of God.

This was not just a prayer made by the minister of our Baptism. The fact is, Baptism actually gives us a power to hear that we did not have before—not a physical power, but the ability to hear and understand words of God to which we would naturally be stone deaf (see Matthew 13:14-16). This is a greater miracle than the cure of physical deafness.

Faith is not just a judgment on our part that something is believable. It is more than a decision to say something is true. What we call the gift of faith is the gift of sharing in God's own knowing act. By faith we know what God knows, and we know it with the certitude God has about it, because we share in God's own act of knowing it. This comes from being united to Jesus Christ as members of his Body, and sharing in his divine life by the gift of grace.

Before this gift a person is like an unlit candle—able to receive light but not yet enlightened. Before we receive the light of Christ (which means before we begin, as members of his Body, to share with him in his own act of knowing), we can no more hear the truth of Jesus' divine teaching than we can see without eyes. We are not equipped to understand or believe truths on the level of God. We might decide to accept some of the teachings in the gospel, and hold to them with human conviction, but this is not the same as the absolute adherence of faith. And some truths—like the doctrine of the cross and love for enemies who are oppressing and killing us—would be utterly beyond us (see 1 Corinthians 1:18-31). Even with the gift of faith we need to pray deeply to accept all of the teaching of Jesus. That is because faith is the act of seeing what God alone can see. It is a power to hear which we can only have through surrender—surrender to his light, his love, his life.

An immeasurable amount of the evil, the pain and suffering in this world comes from the fact that Christians who can hear do not listen or speak out. We who have received the light of faith do not use it to look through the eyes of Christ at the realities of our time. Saint James reproached the early Christians for discriminating between the rich and the poor (see James 2:1-5). We discriminate between blacks and whites; between immigrant ethnic groups and the established social class; between non-threatening sinners to be converted and dangerous criminals to be executed; between loved ones to be protected and enemies to be destroyed in war. We discriminate between our own national interests and the aspirations of impoverished, deprived peoples. And because we do not show the same loving concern for the bad and the good, the just and the unjust, for those who are close to us and those who are not (see Matthew 5: 38-48), we do not bear the witness on earth that we should bear to the way of truth Christ taught. We do not lead. That is probably the one greatest reason for the crisis the world is in right now.

This crisis moved Pope John XXIII to convene Vatican Council II. He attributed the crisis of our times to the fact that people are trying to "reorganize society without God." Who are these people? Not just the Communists, the Arab terrorists and the I.R.A., but all who are trying to solve problems and promote their interests without the light of Christ—in business and politics, in family and recreational life. The world is in darkness because it is trying to see without light, and the blind are leading the blind because those who have the power to see and to hear will not lead them. That is why we need to be disciples.

Reflecting on This Week's Gospels

Twenty-Third Week of the Year

> *Pray daily: Lord, you opened my ears at Baptism. Now open my heart that I might understand all I hear and live out all I understand. Let me increase the light of your truth in the world*

Monday: Luke 6:6-11. Looking around at them all, he then said to him, "Stretch out your hand." Do you want to "stretch out" your heart and be challenged by Jesus' words? Or do you just want to keep "in bounds"?

Tuesday: Luke 6:12-19. Everyone sought to touch him because power came forth from him and healed them all. What power do you believe Jesus has for you? How do you seek to touch him? When? How is he available to you?

Wednesday: Luke 6:20-26. "Woe to you who are full now, / for you will be hungry." What makes you feel most fulfilled? For what do you hunger? When do your efforts to fill yourself leave you most empty?

Thursday: Luke 6:27-38. "[G]ive, and it will be given to you. A good measure, pressed down, shaken together, running over, will be put into your lap; for the measure you give will be the measure you get back." Do you experience the joy and power of Christ's grace in abundance? How much time do you give to learning from him?

Friday: Luke 6:39-42. "Why do you see the speck in your neighbor's eye, but do not notice the log in your own eye?" When you judge others for their faults, which is worse: what you are seeing or what you are doing? Do you look in yourself for the roots of the same faults that you see in others?

Saturday: Luke 6:43-49. "Why do you call me, 'Lord, Lord,' and do not do what I tell you?" How often each day do you consciously think of something Jesus himself taught?

What could you do to make yourself more conscious of
his teachings?

Living This Week's Gospels

As Christian: Consciously make an act of faith in
everything Jesus teaches. Then ask Jesus to be your
Teacher of life. Invite him seriously.

As Disciple: Spell out—in terms of time and space—
what you, on your part, are willing to do in order to
learn from Jesus.

As Prophet: Write down three things you accept as the
teaching of Jesus which are on a higher level of idealism
than common Church teaching requires you to accept. If
you cannot find three, make some choices.

As Priest: Make a point of not discriminating against
anyone because of race or ethnic origin. Take one step to
break through the separation that you inherited from society.

As King: Ask what would be different in your work, social
life or family if you constantly brought everything you do
under the light of Christ's teachings. Take a step toward
changing something.

Power That Saves

Isaiah 50:4-9; James 2:14-18; Mark 8:27-35

What power does Jesus use to save us? When he revealed his plan for saving the world, it appeared to be the renunciation of all power: "undergo great suffering...be rejected...be killed." His refusal to use divine power against evil people the way everyone expected was such a shock to the Apostles that Peter felt it was his duty to take Jesus aside and counsel him.

To understand what power Jesus chooses to use and not use, we have to be clear about his purpose. For Jesus, to "save the world" means to change people. It does not mean, first and foremost, to change the situation. This is why the divine power he chooses to use is the power of love. It is love which converts people from the heart. Any other kind of power may succeed in changing people's behavior, but only love can win people to conversion—at least to the kind of conversion God desires. Only love works.

What do we ask of a savior—any kind of savior: a politician, a new manager, a lawyer, a friend-in-need, a therapist, a doctor, a police officer? Don't we normally ask a savior to save us from something beyond our control, something we feel helpless to change? We call for a savior to come in and use some power we do not have to deliver us from something that threatens us. The savior's power may be physical strength or force; it may be knowledge; it may be technique; it may even be connections and influence with other people. But it is a power we do not have, one that can rescue.

Sometimes rescue works. If you are drowning and a lifeguard pulls you ashore, or if your heart stops and a doctor pounds it into action again, the rescuer's use of power has saved your life. But frequently rescue is an illusion. Very often being rescued just encourages us to ignore the cause of our problem. Sometimes we ask people to save us in such a way that the cure becomes worse than the disease.

If what threatens us is due to free human actions, whether others' actions or our own, being "rescued" by power may be an illusion. We may be saved from the immediate consequences of our own bad behavior, or from the behavior of someone who is threatening us, but if we do not do something about the cause of the bad behavior, we are only delaying disaster. The doctor who saves you from your heart attack will tell you that you will have a worse one if you do not change your diet. The therapist who pulls you through a crisis will tell you to expect another one if you do not change your attitudes. The police know they cannot stop crime by arresting criminals; generals know that military victories never bring about lasting peace; good managers know that borrowing more money is not enough to solve financial problems. But we keep depending on doctors to keep us healthy, therapists to keep us happy, the police to keep our streets safe, the military to protect national security, and on the quick fix, financial or otherwise, to solve our immediate problems. We welcome simplistic (or unscrupulous) saviors who bring in expensive equipment to fill in our graves while in fact they are digging them deeper.

Jesus is not a popular savior because he is an honest one. He does not pretend to be saving us by using divine power to change whatever it is in society—whatever it is in other people's behavior—that is threatening us. Jesus tells us plainly that the problems in our world are due to one thing, and one thing only: that we do not love one another. If we will accept to learn from him how to love, the solutions to all our other problems will soon be obvious to us. God has given us the resources, both material and intellectual, to make human life healthy and happy on earth. But love must be our guiding principle. Selfishness destroys; love gives life.

The only power Jesus promises to use for us is the power that enables us to love as he loves. This is the only power that saves.

Reflecting on This Week's Gospels

Twenty-Fourth Week of the Year

> *Pray daily: Lord, I believe in you as the only true Savior of the world. Teach me to believe in the love you showed us as the only true power against evil. Teach me to love others as you have loved me.*

Monday: Luke 7:1-10. "I am not worthy to have you come under my roof.... For I also am a man set under authority, with soldiers under me;...and I say...to my slave, 'Do this,' and the slave does it." Do you see as much need for authority in the Church as in other human endeavors?

Tuesday: Luke 7:11-17. He touched the coffin, and he said, "Young man, I say to you, rise!" How does your dying to self give Jesus the power to raise you from the dead? Is this just bodily death?

Wednesday: Luke 7:31-35. "[W]isdom is vindicated by all her children." Have Christians throughout history proved the value of Jesus' way of saving the world by consistently choosing love over force, and martyrdom rather than violence? How are you proving it?

Thursday: Luke 7:36-50. Jesus said to the Pharisee: "A certain creditor had two debtors; one owed five hundred denarii, and the other fifty. When they could not pay, he canceled the debts for both of them. Now which of them will love him more?" Is your confidence in God's love for you based on the fact you are keeping his rules or on the experience of his forgiveness? How do you show your love?

Friday: Luke 8:1-3. Accompanying him were the Twelve and some women who had been cured of evil spirits, Mary, called Magdalene.... How do the sins to which you have "died" bear witness to Christ's power? To his love?

Saturday: Luke 8:4-15. "As for what fell among the thorns, these are the ones who hear; but as they go on their way, they are choked by the cares and riches and pleasures of life, and their fruit does not mature." How would dying to the things you worry about enhance your life?

Living This Week's Gospels

As Christian: Examine the ways you are willing to sacrifice people for the sake of maintaining a better environment for yourself or others (shouting at people who are annoying, approving the death penalty, killing enemies in war to preserve democracy). Compare this with the choice Jesus made.

As Disciple: Look through the Gospels trying to find instances in which Jesus teaches it is legitimate to destroy people in order to keep them from destroying the environment or society in which other people live.

As Prophet: The next time you are in a situation in which you would normally resort to power or force in order to get something done or to prevent injustice to yourself or others, try using patience, respect and love instead.

As Priest: Go out of your way daily to show respect and love for people you live or work with so that if a conflict does arise with someone you can address it from a basis of demonstrated appreciation and care for that person. For example, consistently praise everything you can in every person you deal with.

As King: Examine the policies—established or accepted ways of acting, whether written out or not—where you live and work. Ask if any say, in effect, that maintaining a good environment for the group is more important than any particular individual. Don't oversimplify the question. (How much does a good environment have to do with the good of persons? Do we go against an individual's good by insisting on respect for the group's welfare?)

Twenty-Fifth Sunday of the Year

Jesus as Teacher

Wisdom 2:12, 17-20; James 3:16 to 4:3; Mark 9:30-37

A s disciples of Jesus, we should notice some things about his way of teaching. It will help us learn from him better.

First, he teaches things that cannot be grasped on first bounce. The Gospel tells us that even the twelve who were his picked students did not understand him when he talked about his way of saving the world by dying on the cross—by enduring evil with love. The teachings of Jesus—what we, as his disciples are trying to learn—are too deep, too different from what is taken for granted in this world, too divine for us to just listen to them once and say, "I've got it!" Like Mary, we will only understand if we "keep all these things in our heart," reflecting on them, pondering them, letting them grow to clarity within us (see Luke 2:19, 51).

The Gospel shows us another reason, probably the main reason, why his disciples failed to understand Jesus—and still do. "They were afraid" to question him more deeply. There are some things we do not ask about or think about deeply because we are afraid of what the answer might be.

We do not want to saw off a limb we're sitting on! If we depend on something, or think we do, for our survival, to keep our jobs or our friends, we do not want to cut that out of our lives. At the time of the Civil War the Christians who could not understand that slavery was wrong were the ones who lived in states which depended on slave labor. The Northerners were not smarter than the Southerners, or better Christians; they just did not depend on slavery, and so they could see it was wrong. Industrialists who pollute the atmosphere are not dumber than environmentalists, or greater sinners. They just have a lot to lose by keeping the air clean, and so they do not see how important it is. The same is true of people who depend on those industries for their jobs. And we can be sure there is a lot Jesus teaches which we do not understand, just because what he seems to say does not appear to be in our interest. That is the reason we do not ask ourselves what he really means, or reflect on his teaching deeply.

There are plenty of ways to express our love for God and for others without getting into ways which might call for changes in our lives. There is plenty to study in the teaching of Jesus without taking up the hard questions. We can prune little branches off our lives forever without cutting off any limb we are sitting on! We can give so much time to devotional practices which express the faith we already have that we do not have any left over for deep, challenging discipleship. The best way not to understand what Jesus teaches is just not to ask him any questions—at least, not when we do not want to hear the answers.

What does Jesus do when we do not accept his teaching? When his disciples, for example, were arguing about who was more important, how did Jesus respond? He did not just tell them they were wrong. He held up a higher ideal, an exciting new idea. "Anyone who wants to be first needs to be last, and to be at the service of all." Jesus did not tell the people of his time, "It is wrong for you to have slaves." He taught them that if they were reborn by grace, and accepted God as their Father, then they were brothers and sisters of one another. When our behavior falls short, Jesus gives us a thought to ponder, a deep new principle to incorporate into our lives.

And finally, he gives us something human, like a role model, or an inspiring example—a visible image we can keep before our eyes. To teach his disciples to be last and at the service of all, he put his arms around a little child and said, "If, as my disciples, you accept a little child like this, you are accepting me—and the One who sent me." That is a picture to keep in our minds. And as the proverb says, one picture is worth a thousand words.

Reflecting on This Week's Gospels

Twenty-Fifth Week of the Year

> *Pray daily: Lord, I believe you are the Teacher of life. I want to know all you teach. I want to accept it and live it. Give me enough trust in you to face the hard sayings in your Gospel and apply them to my life. And give me grace to live them.*

Monday: Luke 8:16-18. "For nothing is hidden that will not be disclosed, nor is anything secret that will not become known and come to light." Which will appear worse: others' sins against you or your refusal to forgive?

Tuesday: Luke 8:19-21. "My mother and my brothers are those who hear the word of God and do it." How does your forgiving others make Jesus see you as intimately united with himself? Is this identification with him sufficient payment for all the evil you have suffered?

Wednesday: Luke 9:1-6. "Wherever they do not welcome you, as you are leaving that town shake the dust off your feet as a testimony against them." Why would anyone not welcome the bearers of Jesus' good news? When have you last rejected some ideal you read or heard preached? Why did you reject it?

Thursday: Luke 9:7-9. Herod the tetrarch heard about all that was happening, and he was greatly perplexed. How often do you feel perplexed at something Jesus said or did? Should this be a frequent experience if you are taking him seriously? How often do you look at what he said and did?

Friday: Luke 9:18-22. "The Son of Man must undergo great suffering, and be rejected by the elders, chief priests, and scribes, and be killed, and on the third day be raised." Why?

Saturday: Luke 9:43-45. "The Son of Man is going to be betrayed into human hands." But [the disciples] did not understand this saying; its meaning was hidden from them. Do you understand why Jesus, who is God, would let himself be betrayed and handed over to arrogant enemies, to be treated any way they desired, and not retaliate? What is the meaning in this?

Living This Week's Gospels

As Christian: Reflect on the words of John Paul II: "Jesus' way of acting and his words, his deeds and his precepts constitute the moral rule of Christian life" (*The Splendor of Truth*, #20). Can you accept this for yourself, as your standard of morality?

As Disciple: List from memory as many hard sayings of Jesus as you can think of. Observe the feelings you have in reaction to each one.

As Prophet: Take one of the hard sayings you thought of and think about it until you see a practical way to apply it to your own life. Do it.

As Priest: Think of some of the hard things you have to say to others (friends, employees, children, students). How can you say them with the gentleness of Jesus? By making them inspiring? By example?

As King: Ask if there is any situation at home, at work, among your friends, which you have avoided addressing because you are afraid of the consequences. Think seriously about what you should do.

Twenty-Sixth Sunday of the Year

Is Truth Important?

Numbers 11:25-29; James 5:1-6; Mark 9:38-48

J esus tells his disciples not to worry if someone not visibly united to them is working miracles in his name. "Anyone who is not against us is for us," he tells them.

Finally Christians have begun to follow this teaching. We do not condemn people of other denominations, or even of non-Christian religions, like we used to. We respect any sign of good will in each other. Catholics read Protestant authors and vice versa. We accept a non-Christian like Mohandas Ghandi as someone whose insight into Jesus' teaching about nonviolence may be clearer than our own. We are willing to learn from anyone who studies Jesus and whose life bears witness to love of God. Humility is truth, and to be open to truth, wherever it comes from, is humility.

But Jesus adds, "If anyone leads people away from the truth, that person would be better off dead!" Jesus does not take truth lightly. Truth guides action, and our actions lead us either toward the fullness of life or toward the emptiness of a death that is more than the death of the body. To die to truth and goodness and to deep, vital relationship with Christ is to die to everything that lasts, everything that really is. It is to die to the goodness of our own existence.

People still say, "It does not make any difference what you believe as long as you are sincere." This is absurd. Does it make no difference what doctors believe about health care so long as they are sincere? Or what politicians believe is good for the country so long as they are sincere? Or what bankers believe is a good investment, so long as they are sincere? Sincerity frees us from guilt, but it does not free us from the consequences of our choices. And the consequences, even of sincere bad choices, can be disastrous.

We seldom preach about hell anymore. I do not know why others do not, but I have two reasons: First, it is so hard to know when a person (even oneself) has the sufficient knowledge and full consent of the will required for mortal sin, that we cannot just say anymore, as we did in the old days, "If you do this and die without repenting, you are going straight to hell." We still believe and teach that people who die in a state of mortal sin (sin which separates us from Christ and constitutes a rejection of the life of grace) are lost in hell forever. But we cannot say when, in any individual's life, a particular sin is mortal. Nor can we say, if we deliberately do something seriously wrong, that it is not mortal. My advice is, do not take the chance!

The second reason why I seldom, if ever, preach about hell is that my gut feeling (not infallible!) is that this is the time to motivate people by love, not fear. To be honest, I'm glad I had a lot of fear when I was young; I think it kept me out of trouble. But I cannot bring myself to use fear as a motive when I preach today. I hope the people who need fear, as I believe I did, will be able to generate their own!

But I can preach consequences! Leaving aside the question of guilt and mortal sin and hell, it is just a fact that every choice we make creates us, forms us, gives shape to our souls. God creates us as "human beings;" we create ourselves as the unique, individual persons we become. By our choices we write the meaning of our names. We become what we choose. If we lie we become liars. If we hate we become haters. If we just follow our culture we become wimps. And if we "change our minds" *(metanoia)* and repent, we become new again! What we write we can erase and write over, so long as we are alive. Jesus is an open door.

And if we do not understand the truth, our choices will be bad and their effect on other people and on the world around us will be bad. We can wreck our family life, business life, international relations by sincere bad choices. Jesus says it is better to lose anything than to do this, than to lose the truth that guides us well.

Reflecting on This Week's Gospels

Twenty-Sixth Week of the Year

> *Pray daily: Lord, you are the Life and the Light of God, the Savior and the Teacher of life. Help me to understand that by seeing your truth in its fullness I will be able to choose life in its fullness. Call me, motivate me to be your disciple.*

Monday: Luke 9:46-50. "Master, we saw someone casting out demons in your name..." Jesus said, "Do not stop him, for whoever is not against you is for you." Are you willing to forget all divisions and cooperate with anyone who is trying to do something good?

Tuesday: Luke 9:51-56. When the Samaritans would not receive them the disciples asked, "Lord, do you want us to command fire to come down from heaven to consume them?" Jesus rebuked them. What is your spontaneous reaction to rejection? Your chosen response?

Wednesday: Luke 9:57-62. "No one who puts a hand to the plow and looks back is fit for the kingdom of God." How often do you "look back" to previous injuries or insults? Do you find Christ there?

Thursday: Luke 10:1-12. "Whenever you enter a town and its people welcome you, eat what is set before you; cure the sick who are there, and say to them, 'The kingdom of God has come near to you.'" How many times recently have you tried to cure someone (to help someone live more fully) by speaking about something Jesus said, taught or did?

Friday: Luke 10:13-16. "Woe to you, Chorazin! Woe to you, Bethsaida! For if the deeds of power done in you had been done in Tyre and Sidon, they would have repented long ago, sitting in sackcloth and ashes." How do the sins to which you have died bear witness to Christ's power? To his love?

Saturday: Luke 10:17-24. "I thank you, Father, Lord of heaven and earth, because you have hidden these things from the wise and the intelligent and have revealed them to infants." How would dying to the things you worry about enhance your life?

Living This Week's Gospels

As Christian: Think about your call to evangelize. Talk seriously to someone who does not know Christ well enough to want to belong to a church. Invite someone to Mass with you.

As Disciple: Decide what teaching of Jesus or truth about Jesus inspires or helps you the most. What in the Gospel means the most to you? Think about how you could explain this to someone else.

As Prophet: See if you can think of some action you can do which, without words, will express or convey to others what Jesus means to you.

As Priest: Talk to someone of another faith, looking for common ground.

As King: Think of some particular issue which needs to be addressed where you live or work. Speak with one or more other people who might agree with you about it, regardless of their convictions about other things, and see if you can work together to remedy the situation.

The Impossible Life

Genesis 2:18-24; Hebrews 2:9-11; Mark 10:2-16

There is an old Latin proverb: *Ad impossibile nemo tenetur*—"No one is obliged to do the impossible." Since Jesus came this rule no longer applies.

Jesus came, not just to save us from sin—from falling below par in our human lives, but to save us from being confined to the level of human life altogether. He came to call us to live on the level of God. To be saved really means to share in the life of God and to live on the level of God in our thoughts, attitudes, decisions and actions. This is manifestly impossible. But Baptism commits us to it.

We find a good example of this in the Gospel. In answer to a question about divorce Jesus changes the nature of marriage! Until then a "good" marriage was one in which husband and wife made life satisfying for each other on earth. (See the description of the ideal wife in Proverbs 31:10-31. There is no description of the ideal husband; apparently even the Holy Spirit's imagination did not reach that far!) But Jesus establishes a principle which can only be explained if he is changing the goal, and therefore the nature, of marriage.

If divorce is never permitted, then it must be that a "good" marriage, one that is achieving its purpose and doing essentially what a marriage is meant to do, is not one in which the spouses are making life easier for each other, but one in which both spouses are learning to love. Jesus does not guarantee that any two people will always enjoy living together. But he does guarantee that any two people who work at it, using all the means he has provided— reading Scripture and praying together, using Mass and the sacraments—can grow in love for each other. To accept the principle of no divorce, then, is to accept that the goal of marriage is to teach two people to love as God loves; that is, with total unselfishness, in total gift of self. Any marriage which is achieving this, even though it might be far from pleasant, is still a "good" marriage, because it is leading towards its goal: the perfection of love.

Jesus came, then, to make marriage impossible! The goal of Christian marriage is quite simply for both spouses to learn how to love like God, on the level of God—something so high that no human being could possibly stand at the altar and promise with any confidence or credibility at all to achieve it!

This makes Jesus a Savior who makes life impossible! He makes it impossible by changing the goal, the level of life to which we are called. But he makes it possible by giving us a share in his own life, giving us the power to live on the level of God, which is what the word grace means. A Christian marriage is possible if both spouses work at it with Jesus, guided by his words, strengthened by his sacraments, in response to his Spirit, living fully the life of grace.

To be saved, then, means, not just to be saved from sin, but to be lifted up to a whole new level of life: God's level; to accept a whole new framework of attitudes: God's attitudes; and to live by a whole new set of values and priorities: God's values, God's priorities. It means to be called to something beyond human power and at the same time to be enabled to do it. It means to be called to the "perfection of love"—not only in marriage, but in our social life, business life, political and civic involvement. We have to love like Christ in everything we do. That is the only goal we really have to accomplish (see John 15:12).

This gives new meaning to the word Savior. Jesus as Savior is someone we need all the time, in everything we do. We need to be constantly united with him in mind and heart in order to succeed in doing anything in the way we are called to do it.

Reflecting on This Week's Gospels

Twenty-Seventh Week of the Year

Pray daily: Lord, you are the Teacher of life and of love. Give me the grace to believe in your way, to study it in your words, and to follow it to life to the full.

Monday: Luke 10:25-37. "You shall love the Lord with all your heart, and with all your soul, and with all your strength, and with all your mind." How does this commandment turn every dying to self into an increase of life? What experiences of sacrificing yourself in the past have not enhanced your life? Did you do them out of love? What sacrifices have you made out of love? Did they bring you to life?

Tuesday: Luke 10:38-42. "Martha, you are worried and distracted by many things; there is need of only one thing." What is the one thing necessary? Do you direct everything in your life toward this?

Wednesday: Luke 11:1-4. "And forgive us our sins, / for we ourselves forgive everyone indebted to us." How does dying to hurts and wrongs through forgiveness make us more alive?

Thursday: Luke 11:5-13. "Ask, and it will be given you; search and you will find; knock and the door will be opened for you." Do you seek and knock as much as you ask? For what?

Friday: Luke 11:15-26. "Whoever is not with me is against me, and whoever does not gather with me scatters." To be "with" Christ, is it enough just to be not against him—not to be doing anything wrong? What makes you positively with him at home? At work? In your social life? When are you "scattered"?

Saturday: Luke 11:27-28. A woman called out, "Blessed is the womb that bore you...." He replied, "Blessed rather are those who hear the word of God and obey it." What do you admire most in Mary? What do you do to imitate her?

Living This Week's Gospels

As Christian: Ask what does or would express daily in your life that you are with Christ, seeking the one thing necessary, making perfect love the goal of your life.

As Disciple: If a stranger looked at all the books and magazines in your house, what would appear to be your main interest in life? What would say you are a disciple of Christ?

As Prophet: Identify three concrete things you did during the past week which indicate that loving God and others is your highest priority in life. Rejoice in them.

As Priest: List in order of priority the five people you nurture or minister to the most. (Think of family, neighborhood, work, church, social life, city or country.)

As King: Think of one thing that people around you do that you would like to change. On one side of a piece of paper list all the ways you could bring about the change this using power or threats. On the other side list all the ways you could change them using love.

What Jesus Asks Is Worth All

Wisdom 7:7-11; Hebrews 4:12-13; Mark 10:17-30

The story of the rich young man is one of the most misunderstood passages in Scripture. For centuries Catholics have been explaining the words, "Go, sell what you own, and give the money to the poor" as a call to take the vow of poverty in a monastery or religious order. Jesus does not require all Christians to give up their property, they argued, so this must be just a counsel, an exhortation to do the "better thing" for those who want to be "perfect."

This established a two-track Christianity: the perfection track ("way of the counsels") for first-string Christians who committed themselves by the religious vows of poverty, celibacy and obedience to doing everything Jesus urged; and the salvation track ("way of the commandments") for the laity, who just aimed at doing what God commanded. Parish ministry was geared to helping the laity get to heaven, not to get really holy or intimate with God. Vatican II changed all this by declaring that the "perfection of love" is the aim of every authentic Christian way of life. To take our baptismal vows seriously is to be embarked on a way of perfection, because there is no two-track Christianity in the Gospels, but only the way of total gift which Jesus taught to all.

The truth is that Jesus' response here is neither a command nor a counsel, but an example. It is one thing a person might do to enter into the kingdom of God; one thing among many that can let us experience and know that we have entered into conscious, deep relationship with Jesus Christ. To give everything away to the poor is a dramatic gesture of passionate love. Jesus teaches that this gesture—or one like it—is that "one more thing you must do" if you want to experience your religion for what it truly is: a relationship of passionate love for Jesus Christ.

And this is what Christianity is. Our religion is not just a religion of rules or routine. We are not good Christians, or Catholics who truly know what the Church is all about, just because we keep all the commandments and go to Mass every Sunday. How many young people who can say, "I have kept all the commandments since my childhood" have dropped out of the Church and stopped being active Christians because, as they put it, "It just did not mean anything to me!" Their religion did not mean anything to them because it was not deep, experienced relationship with Jesus Christ. And it was not the Catholic religion either; it was a religion of rules and routine without a soul. It was Christianity without Christ—or without deeply experienced personal relationship with Christ.

To "sell everything" is not an exhortation addressed only to those who want to be special Christians bucking for canonization. Jesus presents this as the entrance exam for becoming his disciples; for beginning to follow him! The way to understand what Jesus Christ is all about is to make some dramatic gesture, right from the start, of giving up in our hearts everything that is in competition with him: money, home, family, marriage, even life itself. (For other examples see Luke 9:23-27; 12:49-53; 14:26; Matthew 19:10-12, 29; 16:24-28).

Does this seem extreme? Isn't this exactly what every married couple does? Anyone who marries gives up every other man or woman on earth for the sake of one spouse. The married leave home and parents. They put all their possessions at the service of each other and of their children. They would give up all they possess and even their lives, if necessary, to help each other. And this passionate, total gift of self to each other is expressed in the passionate self-giving of sexual intercourse. All love is gift. Total love is total gift. And the love we learn from Jesus Christ is passionate, total gift. To accept Jesus on these terms is the only way to understand him.

Reflecting on This Week's Gospels

Twenty-Eighth Week of the Year

Pray daily: Lord, you love me without bounds and you showed it. Teach me how to show you that my love for you is without bounds.

Monday: Luke 11:29-32. "The queen of the South will rise...with the people of this generation and condemn them, because she came from the ends of the earth to listen to the wisdom of Solomon, and see, something greater than Solomon is here." What sacrifices do you make to hear the wisdom of Jesus? What chances are offered in your parish?

Tuesday: Luke 11:37-41. "Now you Pharisees clean the outside of the cup and of the dish, but inside you are full of greed and wickedness." What specific ways are offered to you in the parish to help you purify, clarify, lift higher the attitudes and values in your heart?

Wednesday: Luke 11:42-46. "[W]oe to you Pharisees! For you tithe... and neglect justice and the love for God." What do you see as the basic obligations of your religion? What do you see as "good but extra"? In which list do you put participating in Scripture study, discussion groups, retreats? What, concretely, are you doing to grow in understanding God's heart?

Thursday: Luke 11:47-54. "Therefore also the Wisdom of God said, 'I will send them prophets...some of whom they will kill....'" What efforts have been made in your parish to teach you more about the Gospel? Have you voted to kill these initiatives by just not participating? How have you supported them?

Friday: Luke 12:1-7. "Do not fear those who kill the body, and after that can do nothing more." Do you worry more about losing your physical fitness, than you do about just not growing in knowledge and love of God? Is a smoke-free environment more important to you than a bad-value-free environment?

Saturday: Luke 12:8-12. "Everyone who acknowledges me before others, the Son of Man also will acknowledge before the angels of God." What visible actions in your life say, not just that you believe in Jesus, but that you love him above everything else life offers?

Living This Week's Gospels

As Christian: List what is offered in the parish to help you experience God (daily Mass, Reconciliation, study groups). Then list the reasons you do not use them more. Compare the values on both sides.

As Disciple: List the religious duties you perform faithfully. Underline those which are changing your attitudes and values.

As Prophet: Write "from the ends of the earth" on a card (see Monday) and do one thing each day to embody that priority.

As Priest: At daily Mass or at home offer yourself with Jesus lifted up on the cross for others. Then give life through love.

As King: Drop your pastor a note affirming one thing that says the parish is aiming at more than routine religion—or suggesting one thing he could do that would say this.

Twenty-Ninth Sunday of the Year

Jesus Gives Giving

Isaiah 53:10-11; Hebrews 4:14-16; Mark 10:35-45

In the beginning Jesus' disciples thought Jesus came to save the world the way we would like to see a president save the United States: by doing away with unjust laws, stopping crime and oppression, establishing prosperity and securing peace. They also assumed, naturally, that anyone who worked closely with Jesus to bring this about would enjoy a position of power and prestige in his kingdom. Big mistake.

Two of them, James and John, Zebedee's sons, asked Jesus specifically for this, and his answer to them gives all of us a key to what it means to be saved. What kind of Savior is Jesus? What does he save us from? How do we know we have truly accepted his salvation?

Jesus tells them that rewards of power and prestige are not his to give. What he can share with them is his cup— the cup of labor, rejection and pain that will come to him as Savior of the world. What Jesus offers us as Savior is a share in what he does as Savior. And what he does as Savior is sacrifice himself for the good of others. The privilege of doing this with him is the glory he offers to his followers here on earth.

What about afterwards? If we sacrifice ourselves for others during this life, can we look forward to a reward of glory in heaven?

Yes, but we need to understand what that glory is. It is glory like our Lord's own glory. And our Lord's glory in heaven is not just the glory he had with the Father before the world began (see John 17:5). It is also the glory of what he became through his human life, the glory he entered into through his passion and death. The glory of Jesus is simply what he is, revealed to the world in all its beauty. This includes what he became through coming to this earth, "not to be served but to serve," and to give his life for the life of us all.

The point is that what Jesus offers us as Savior on this earth and what he offers us in heaven are essentially one and the same thing. He offers to share his life with us ("the grace of our Lord Jesus Christ"). On earth this life shows itself as the divine love that is revealed in our sacrifice of self for others. In heaven this same life shows itself as our glory; that is, as the beauty of what we have become through giving ourselves for others in love.

What is the key to being saved? Well, of course, it is believing in Jesus as the Savior of the world. But what does it mean to believe in him as Savior? It means to believe both in what he is as God-made-man and in what he does as God saving the world through human actions.

What Jesus does to save the world is give himself in love—even unto death. And anyone who truly believes in him as Savior must accept both to share his divine life, which is grace, and to live that life on earth as Jesus did, which is to serve the needs of all in constant, self-giving love. In other words, if we want to get practical about what it means to be saved, and to talk about it in terms of concrete actions, it means to focus all the time on what we can do for others rather than on what we can get out of others or get others to do for us. And it means to do this, not just as benevolent humanitarians, but as sharers in the life and mission of Jesus who came to give his life that others might have "life to the full" (see John 10:10).

What kind of Savior is Jesus? A Savior who saves us by enabling us to become something better than we are. What does he save us from? Self-centeredness. He saves us from making ourselves the goal of all we do. And how do we know we have accepted his salvation? When we find ourselves seeking, not to be served but to serve and to give our lives that others might live the life of grace in its fullness.

Reflecting on This Week's Gospels

Twenty-Ninth Week of the Year

> *Pray daily: Lord, you came to give me the power to give love every moment of my life. I was made for love, redeemed for love, consecrated to love. Teach me to love to the full.*

Monday: Luke 12:13-21. "Take care! Be on your guard against all kinds of greed; for one's life does not consist in the abundance of possessions." What five things in your house do you use most? Is the Bible one of them?

Tuesday: Luke 12:35-38. "Be dressed for action and have your lamps lit; be like those who are waiting for their master to return from the wedding banquet, so that they may open the door for him as soon as he comes and knocks." Do you recognize it as Jesus knocking when you are called upon to sacrifice yourself for others? Do you rejoice in it?

Wednesday: Luke 12:39-48. "From everyone to whom much has been given, much will be required; and from the one to whom much has been entrusted, even more will be demanded." How much money has been entrusted to you? Education? Skill? Charm? Health? How much are you doing for the Kingdom of God with each?

Thursday: Luke 12:49-53. "I came to bring fire to the earth, and how I wish it were already kindled!" What are you most excited about or passionately involved in right now? Will it matter to you in heaven? How much passion do you have to make God known?

Friday: Luke 12:54-59. "You know how to interpret the appearance of earth and sky, but why do you not know how to interpret the present time?" Do you listen to weather reports? Financial reports? The news? Why? How much time each day do you spend keeping conscious of things that affect your spiritual future? What would help you do this?

Saturday: Luke 13:1-9. "For three years I have come looking for fruit on this fig tree, and still I find none." What are the five most loving things you have done for God in the past three years? What are you doing now to increase this over the next three years?

Living This Week's Gospels

As Christian: Consciously accept Jesus as your Savior who saves precisely by calling you to give up your life to loving.

As Disciple: List what you think should be your priorities in acquiring information or knowledge. Ask how you can make these your priorities in reality—that is, in action?

As Prophet: Each day this week give witness to God by some use of your possessions, time and energy that only makes sense in the light of faith.

As Priest: Write the names of the flock entrusted to your care. What are you doing to shepherd them? To nourish them with light, love?

As King: Where is love most lacking around you? Decide on one step you can take to begin to change this.

Thirtieth Sunday of the Year

To Accept Jesus Is to Want to See

Jeremiah 31:7-9; Hebrews 5:1-6; Mark 10:46-52

For Jesus to save us, we have to really want to be saved. That is why he asks the blind man in today's Gospel, "What do you want me to do for you?" When the man answered, "I want to see," is it really certain he was answering for us all?

If Jesus appeared to you today and asked, "What three things would you like me to do for you?" would one of the three be, "Lord, let me see things as you do; change the way you think!"?

When you think of Jesus as "saving" you, do you think of him as teaching you new attitudes and values? Inviting you to change your most fundamental assumptions about life? Or do you think of him just as helping you to live up to the ideals you already have, or to avoid the sins you already see as bad?

Not all of our sins come from weakness of will. Some come from darkness of intellect, not seeing the picture clearly. The first of the "Twelve Steps" of Alcoholics Anonymous is simply to see and admit that one's life has become unmanageable because of alcohol. When we honestly "want to see" why we cannot stop drinking, or sinning in any compulsive way, we are on the road to recovery.

Why, for example, do we lose our patience so often? Is it because we just don't have a lot of self-control? Or because we approach people and life and responsibilities out of some attitude which sets us up for impatience?

Jesus saves us—or offers to save us—from unrecognized attitudes born of the unblessed mating of our culture and our minds. Just as true marriages are based on conscious, free consent to enter into union with another, true "meeting of minds" comes from conscious acceptance of ideas openly offered. What we call "cultural conditioning" is the insertion of ideas into the mind by manipulation and stealth without free or conscious acceptance. It is like being raped in your sleep.

Jesus comes to us frankly proclaiming Himself as the true light of the world, inviting us to accept a "fresh, spiritual way of thinking" (Ephesians 4: 23-24) and to be "transformed" by the renewal of our minds (Romans 12: 2). He tells us honestly that we are blinded by the darkness of this world, by the underlying, universally accepted attitudes, values and prejudices of our culture, and that if we want to be saved we have to begin by praying, "Lord, I want to see."

As Savior Jesus proposes to turn our thinking upside down. He claims to be the "light of the world," the true light which comes from God and which the darkness of our culture (or any culture) cannot overshadow. Jesus claims that his words are spirit and life, and that the truth he teaches can set us free *(see John 1: 1-17; 6: 60-69* and *8: 31-47)*. The question is, do we really believe this?

Do we recognize that we are blind, and do we really want to see?

If we do, we begin to interact with him in a new way. He becomes for us more than the Savior to whom we pray for help. He becomes the Teacher of Life, the "Master of the Way." He becomes the model, the example, of how a human life should be lived on this earth—the image of what our own lives should look like, and what fruits they should bear, of what goals we should focus on. Jesus becomes for us someone we look at before every choice and decision we make, just as an artist looks at the subject of a painting before every stroke of the brush. If we are really saying, "Lord, I want to see," the proof will be that we look. Perhaps the first thing we should pray for, then, is the grace to see that we are blind.

Reflecting on This Week's Gospels

Thirtieth Week of the Year

> *Pray daily: Lord, you open the eyes of the blind: you are the light of the world. Open my eyes, that I might see you and live life to the full.*

Monday: Luke 13:10-17. "This daughter of Abraham, whom Satan has bound for eighteen years now, ought she not to have been set free on the sabbath day from this bondage?" How many years have you been in bondage to cultural attitudes and values? Do you really want to be set free? What role does the sabbath play in this?

Tuesday: Luke 13:18-21. "The kingdom of God is like yeast that a woman took and mixed with three measures of flour until the whole batch of dough was leavened." Can you trace a gradual transformation of your attitudes and values through interaction with Jesus in his Church? Do you try to make this happen?

Wednesday: Luke 13:22-30. "Strive to enter through the narrow door, for many will try to enter but will not be able." Does "being broad-minded" mean accepting persons as equal, or accepting values as equal? Do you ever confuse this in speech or in action?

Thursday: Luke 13:31-35. "Jerusalem, the city that kills the prophets and stones those who are sent to it! How often have I desired to gather your children together as a hen gathers her brood under her wings, and you were not willing!" When, where, in how many ways does Jesus call the Church together today? Are you unwilling?

Friday: Luke 14:1-6. Jesus spoke to the scholars of the law and Pharisees in reply, asking, "'Is it lawful to cure people on the sabbath, or not?' But they were silent." Have you had questions about things you have read in the Scripture or heard preached at Mass? Did you ask about them or seek for answers? Do you prefer to understand everything in your religion or to remain in ignorance?

Saturday: Luke 14:1, 7-11. "All who exalt themselves will be humbled, but those who humble themselves will be exalted." Humility means "being peaceful with the truth." Are you?

Living This Week's Gospels

As Christian: Read Luke 4:16-21, asking how believing this could transform your life.

As Disciple: Read the Sermon on the Mount, underlining what you "want to see."

As Prophet: Write down three things that the teaching of Jesus has made you see and do differently from others in your family life, social life or professional life.

As Priest: Each day this week look for a new way to live out with the people you deal with Jesus' command: "Love one another as I have loved you."

As King: Identify one way of acting in your environment that seems to be based on a different way of seeing things than Jesus teaches. Is there anything you can do about it? (There is always something.)

A Non-Commandment

Deuteronomy 6:2-6; Hebrews 7:23-28; Mark 12:28-34

Jesus really did not say anything new when asked what the greatest commandment was; he just quoted the Old Testament. So what is so special about the teaching of Jesus?

What is special about Jesus' teaching here is not what he added but what he accented. He did not really answer the question as it was asked. He did not pick out one of the commandments as first. Instead he focused attention on the spirit, the soul of all the commandments. He said that what God asks of us—both in our relationship to God and in our relationship with each other—is to love. This is not so much a new law as a new spirit to transform all laws.

It is a common opinion that a law, to be a law, must be enforceable, and that the only way to enforce any law is through fear. That is something to ponder. Some laws we may keep because we happen to agree with them. But when we obey a law precisely as a law, it is because we are afraid of what will happen if we do not—not only to ourselves, but to society in general. Laws are our only protection against chaos. They are the only way for any human society to achieve its goals in a rational, orderly way. Laws defend our national interest. We make them, we keep them, and we enforce them all for the same reason: out of fear of what will happen if we do not.

That is why we imprison or kill people who do not obey the law. They are a threat to us and a threat to society—they destroy the order of things that makes it possible for us to achieve our goals on this earth; to realize our dreams and satisfy our desires. Those who break the law are working against what we have agreed to as a society. We see them as enemies.

When Jesus was asked what law was the most important, he answered that the most important thing was not a law at all—not any law—but love. The most important thing on earth is for people to love God and love one another with their whole hearts. He even taught we should love our enemies. This is what we profess to believe as Christians.

But this is not in fact our first priority—neither as individuals, in most cases, nor as a nation. Our prisons are not designed to rehabilitate people, to teach them, heal them and convert them. Our prisons are not the kind of places to which we would want our children sent if they broke the law. And our defense system, our armies and arms, are not designed to bring about understanding between ourselves and other nations. They are designed to keep others at bay so that we can pursue our national self interest in the way we choose to pursue it. Our prison system and our national defense system are motivated, not by love but by fear. And what percentage of our budget do we spend on them?

Idealistic? Unrealistic? Now we see what was so different about the teaching of Jesus. He came to call us into a whole new mental framework; to challenge and change some of our most fundamental attitudes and assumptions. Is the most important thing for any society to defend itself? Should survival at any cost be our first priority? Should we be agreed as a nation that we will destroy any people who threaten to destroy our established way of life? Which commandment is the most important for us? Is any commandment more important than love? If we cannot enforce the law or defend our nation without destroying other people—physically, economically or psychologically—do we reluctantly accept that our own wellbeing on this earth must take priority over love? Are we agreed as a society, as a nation, that loving one another is a luxury we can allow ourselves only when we have nothing more to fear? Must we wait until our enemies disarm before we love them? Must we wait until the muggers, thieves, rapists and murderers are converted before we love them? Is it really safe to love our enemies? Is being safe the highest value in life? Is being "safe" the same as being "saved"?

Reflecting on This Week's Gospels

Thirty-First Week of the Year

> *Pray daily:* Lord, you gave your life so that those
> guilty of destroying the order of your creation might
> live. You taught us that love, not force, is the only
> true way to save the human race. Teach me to value
> other people more than anything they might take
> from me, even my life. Teach me to love as you love.

Monday: Luke 14:12-14. Then he said to the host who
invited him, "Do not invite your friends or your...relatives
or rich neighbors, in case they may invite you in return,
and you would be repaid. But when you give a banquet,
invite the poor, the crippled, the lame, and the blind."
How much of what you spend on yourself or your family
benefits the poor? The lonely? How could they be included
in everything you do?

Tuesday: Luke 14:15-24. "But they all alike began to make
excuses. The first said to him, 'I have bought a piece of land
and I must go out and see it; please accept my regrets.'
Another said.... Another said...." Would you be on this list?
What keeps you from more serious efforts to learn more
about Christ's teachings? From offering and receiving Christ
at Mass more often? From focusing on God?

Wednesday: Luke 14:25-33. "Whoever comes to me and
does not hate father and mother, wife and children brothers
and sisters, yes, and even life itself cannot be my disciple."
How is this radical statement the same as the radical
commandment to love God with your whole heart and to
love others as Jesus does?

Thursday: Luke 15:1-10. "I tell you, there will be more joy
in heaven over one sinner who repents than over ninety-nine
righteous persons who need no repentance." Which gives you
more satisfaction: that a murderer or rapist should repent of
his crime, or that he should be punished?

Friday: Luke 16:1-8. The master commended that dishonest steward for acting prudently. "For the children of this age are more shrewd in dealing with their own generation than are the children of light." As a Christian, are you willing to do or pay as much to establish the Kingdom of God on earth as you are to maintain civil society? To what extent are they the same? To what extent different?

Saturday: Luke 16:9-15. "No slave can serve two masters; for a slave will either hate one and love the other, or be devoted to the one and despise the other. You cannot serve God and wealth." How much money do you invest in making money? How much time? How much in carrying out the mission of Christ on earth? How much do they overlap in your own particular case?

Living This Week's Gospels

As Christian: Write down the answer to the question, "What are you investing your life in?" Ask a close friend what he or she thinks you are investing your life in. Compare the answers.

As Disciple: Calculate what percentage of your money you spend on taxes, on Church, on your family and friends, on the poor, on yourself. In each category, estimate how much is an expression of love.

As Prophet: See if you can find a way to make everything you spend an explicit expression love for God or other people. Be creative. Work at it gradually.

As Priest: Every time you make a choice, consciously place it on the altar with the bread and wine and ask God to show you how to transform it into an act of love.

As King: Using what you discovered as a "disciple" above, make a "budget report" on how you have used during this liturgical year the resources you have received from God: your gift of faith, the gifts that equip you for ministering to others, and your material resources. Make a proactive budget for next year.

Thirty-Second Sunday of the Year

The Greatest Gift Is You

1 Kings 17:10-16; Hebrews 9:24-28; Mark 12:38-44

It is natural for us to assume that the more we do for God or for the Church, the more religious we are. This comes right out of another assumption, which is just as natural, that the more we are able to do in general, the better human beings we are. As a result, when we are ill, or retired, or just unable for any reason to function very well, we assume that we are not worth very much. A "worthless life" means to us a life that doesn't accomplish anything.

If we think like this, then we will assume that the more we are able to do for God, the better Christians we are. And so we will measure our religion by how much we work for the Church, or how much we give, or perhaps by how many prayers we say. And when we cannot do any of these things, we will assume that we are not worth very much to Jesus.

One of the things Jesus saves us from is this false way of evaluating ourselves. In Mark's Gospel he points out a poor widow who put into the collection box two copper coins worth about one cent. This woman, Jesus says, gave more than anyone else because, "she gave from her want, all she had to live on."

Jesus isn't just saying here that the lady was generous. He is saying that what really matters to him is not what she gives, but what she is. What matters to Jesus is not what we do for him but what we become as persons during our time on earth. The only real and lasting value in anything we do is found in what it helps us or other people become. This is what life is all about. This is what Jesus teaches.

Nothing lasts forever except people. And the joy God takes in his creation is in what human beings become through their responses to the world, to other people, and to him. Everything on earth was created for us, to help us grow to the full likeness of Jesus Christ (see Ephesians 4:11-16). And all that we do on earth, all that we contribute of our time, our talent or our treasure, has no other lasting effect except its effect on ourselves or other people because nothing lasts forever except what we or other people become. The teaching of Jesus about "productivity" or accomplishments is that we should look, not at how much we do or how much we give, but at what we become through the act of doing it or giving it.

There may be fund-raising techniques which "work" in the sense of bringing in money. But achieving the goal of a fund-raising campaign is not achieving the goal of a parish unless in the act of giving people grow closer to Jesus Christ. If increased giving comes from increased understanding of who God is, who we are and what Jesus Christ is all about; and from a clearer, deeper commitment to live for him and take part in his mission on earth, then we have reached our goal.

Are those people more religious, then, who do more or give more to the Church and to other people? It depends. One way to become more loving (which is what being religious is all about) is to do things for other people. To give money, time or energy to support those good works which help people realize their potential as human beings and as children of God, is certainly a way to grow in love. And if being involved in the parish means that we become more aware of needs that have to be met in our world and more willing to meet them, then our parish is helping us grow in love.

But more important than what we do is what we become. That is why our first concern in religion should be to grow in knowledge of Jesus Christ; to become familiar with his words and his example, and to pattern our own lives on everything he said and did. Everything else we do should flow out of this. The best contribution we can make to our parish is simply to grow in likeness to the heart of Jesus Christ. This is our first gift to him and to the world.

Reflecting on This Week's Gospels

Thirty-Second Week of the Year

Pray daily: Lord, you gave me the gift of life and all that goes with it. Show me how to give myself to others and to you.

Monday: Luke 17:1-6. "Occasions for stumbling are bound to come, but woe to anyone by whom they come!" Do any of your words or actions express an ideal lower than what Jesus teaches? Does this concern you?

Tuesday: Luke 17:7-10. "When you have done all that you were ordered to do, say, 'We are worthless slaves; we have done only what we ought to have done!'" What do you owe to God, to Jesus, to the Church, to others?

Wednesday: Luke 17:11-19. "Were not ten made clean? ...Was none of them found to return and give praise to God except this foreigner?" How often do you thank God for all that you receive?

Thursday: Luke 17:20-25. "The days are coming when you will long to see one of the days of the Son of Man, and you will not see it." What opportunities do you have to learn more about Jesus that you may someday kick yourself for not using?

Friday: Luke 17:26-37. "Those who try to make their life secure will lose it, but those who lose their life will keep it." What concrete things do you do to have security in life? How much time, energy, money do you invest in growing to that "life to the full" that Jesus came to give?

Saturday: Luke 18:1-8. "When the Son of Man comes, will he find faith on earth?" What signs of faith are visible in your life that give consolation to Christ? Do they show a faith worthy of him, the kind of faith he deserves?

Living This Week's Gospels

As Christian: Ask yourself, "Is there anything in my life that I have not given to Christ?" Think about it.

As Disciple: Go through the main activities of your day or life, asking how each one helps you to grow, what each one has helped you to become.

As Prophet: Each time you hear someone praised or notice some special sign of respect given to someone, ask yourself what value is being recognized here. If appropriate, ask the one giving the respect.

As Priest: Write an admiring note or say something affirmative to someone who does not qualify for special respect by the ordinary norms applied in our culture.

As King: Evaluate what you contribute to your parish. Is the amount you give based on your knowledge of the need the parish has for money, or on your desire to give explicitly to God "off the top" a certain percentage of your income?

Thirty-Third Sunday of the Year

A Savior Who Lasts

Daniel 12:1-3; Hebrews 10:11-14; Mark 13:24-32

I was talking once to a young man who had been converted to Jesus by a prayer group. He wanted to join the Catholic Church.

"Why is that?" I asked him. "None of the people who helped you find Jesus is a Catholic."

"No," he said, "but since I was saved three years ago I've seen three churches start and stop. I want one that's going to be around for awhile."

Jesus says in the Gospel, "Heaven and earth will pass away, but my words will not pass away." He also says that his Body on earth, the Church, will last until the end of time. Though trials of every kind come, though the sun be darkened and the moon stop giving light, the Church will still be here when Jesus comes at the end. No matter what trials she suffers or temptations she succumbs to, she will survive. History already bears witness to that.

Jesus is putting his followers on guard against our very natural human inclination to get discouraged and to look for instant saviors when things do not go well. Jesus, the true Savior of the world, did not appear to have done anything at all by the time he died. And year after year, following his Resurrection, the Church grew only slowly and very unimpressively. Those who looked to Jesus, or to the community of faith, for a "promised land" of instant relief from anxiety, temptation or struggle looked in vain. Belonging to the community of the Church did not make everything easy and inspiring. It still doesn't. What Jesus taught his followers was that those who persevered to the end would be saved. The People of Israel got to the promised land by going through the desert. There's a lesson in that.

"Being saved" does not relieve us from anger, doubts, the humiliation of falling repeatedly into sin, or the strain of living and praying with others who are even more sinful (in our eyes at least) than we are. Being in the community of the saved, or in the "right" church does not mean that we find the preaching consistently inspiring, the congregation warm and loving, the liturgy beautiful, or the community without sin. Being saved means we believe in Jesus Christ and have the grace to persevere in his Church through all the ups and downs, trials and tribulations, victories and failures, lights and darknesses that may characterize our given period in history. Being saved means having the grace to be faithful— that is, full of faith though the sun be darkened and the moon stop giving light.

Let's face the reality of our times. Vatican II shook up the Church. The Council changed the pattern of our routines and called us to look more deeply, with clearer vision, at what we believe. When we as a Church did this, we held up to each other new hopes, new ideals. And we created new desires.

Those desires are not instantly satisfied, any more than our hopes and ideals are instantly realized. In the liturgy, for example, the change to English opened up great possibilities for full, conscious, active participation at Mass. But we do not always reach this ideal. As a result, some have left the Church to join the "pop-up" churches whose enthusiasm in worship is their best, and sometimes their only, claim to credibility. They think that because they find it easy to feel devotion in these churches they must be saved. Jesus taught the opposite: feeling devotion does not mean you are saved, and being saved does not necessarily mean you will feel devotion. Persevering in faith with hope and with love is the only way to be saved. Being turned on in church does not mean you are in the right one. It might just mean you got there on Opening Day. The test of a church, and of your own faith, is in whether or not you both are still there on Closing Day. What determines that is the way we live the days in between.

Reflecting on This Week's Gospels

Thirty-Third Week of the Year

Pray daily: Lord Jesus, you came that we might "have life, and have it to the full." Let this desire of yours fill my heart. Fill me with desire to open myself to your life and to share it with others.

Monday: Luke 18:35-43. Jesus asked him, "What do you want me to do for you?" He replied, "Lord, let me see again." What do you want Jesus to do for you? What do you want most for yourself? Is it the best?

Tuesday: Luke 19:1-10. Zacchaeus could not see Jesus because of the crowd, "So he ran ahead and climbed a sycamore tree to see him." What efforts do you make to see Jesus in spite of the crowd around him?

Wednesday: Luke 19:11-20. "To all those who have, more will be given; but from those who have nothing, even what they have will be taken away." How do you use what you have—Reconciliation, Eucharist, Scripture, all that is offered to you in your parish?

Thursday: Luke 19:41-44. "The days will come upon you, when your enemies will set up ramparts around you and surround you, and hem you in on every side...because you did not recognize the time of your visitation from God." What evils in our society would not exist if we Christians simply lived what we believe?

Friday: Luke 19:45-48. " 'My house shall be a house of prayer'; / but you have made it a den of robbers." What words would describe what we have made of God's house? What is it apt for? Used for? How effectively? How often?

Saturday: Luke 20:27-40. "He is God not of the dead, but of the living; for to him all of them are alive." How do you experience God, the living God, interacting with you in your life now?

Living This Week's Gospels

As Christian: Write, "I believe in Jesus Christ because..." and complete the sentence. Then write, "I believe in the Church because..." and complete that one.

As Disciple: Read Vatican II's document "The Church" (*Lumen Gentium*) or "The Church in the Modern World" (*Gaudium et Spes*).

As Prophet: Listen to all the words the priest reads at Mass as if you were saying them yourself. Make them the expression of your own response to God.

As Priest: At the Offertory of the Mass, offer yourself with the bread and wine to be transformed more fully into the Body of Christ. At the Consecration/Elevation actively offer Jesus to the Father for the needs of the world; and offer yourself in him and with him.

As King: Ask yourself what would make it easier for you and others to participate "fully, actively, and consciously" in the Mass as it is celebrated in your parish. Talk to your pastor or to someone on the Liturgy Committee about it.

Thirty-Fourth Sunday of the Year (Christ the King)

Jesus Is the Way
to Friendship With God

Daniel 7:13-14; Revelation 1:5-8; John 18: 33-37

D oes it seem odd that on the feast of Christ the King
we focus on Jesus as friend? Friends are people we
feel close to, intimate with. Kings are people we
treat with distant respect.

But when Jesus proclaimed his kingship he was a
prisoner, alone and powerless. He identified his kingship
with "testifying to the truth." He only counted as his
subjects those "committed to the truth." To accept Jesus as
King means to want to know him! "Anyone committed to
the truth hears my voice." Commitment to Christ the King
is commitment to listening to his heart.

What is friendship? Friendship is to be one heart
and mind with another. (Love is to act toward another in a
way that leads to this). When two people feel comfortable
and at home with the truth of what each other is, they are
experiencing friendship. Friendship is rejoicing in the
truth of what each is.

This is what Jesus asks of us. The heaven he designed
for the human race is just people rejoicing in what God is
and what they have become through knowing and loving
him. This is the "reign of Christ"—people being comfortable
in the truth of what Jesus is and they are (see John 17:3).

For the reign of Christ to be established, two things are
required: Jesus' revelation of Himself to our hearts, and our
enthusiastic response to that revelation. Jesus reigns when
truth is established between ourselves and him. "Anyone
committed to the truth hears my voice." Anyone who fully
accepts the truth rejoices in it.

People expected the Messiah to enter the world with

power and subject everything to Himself. Jesus said that he came into the world "to testify to the truth." We understand Christ the King when we understand that these are one and the same. He does not "conquer," "subject" and "dominate." He just reveals himself. If we accept the truth of what he is and rejoice in it, we are under his reign because we are under the reign of truth. They are one and the same.

How can we accept Jesus as King? The only way is to accept him opening his heart, offering to reveal his innermost thoughts to us. He offers us friendship, intimacy and love. It is the only way he accepts to reign. To accept Jesus as intimate friend is the only way we can accept him as Christ the King (see John 6:14-40).

Which would you rather have? Jesus as King or Jesus as intimate friend? Don't be too quick to say "friend." Would you rather have Jesus use his divine power to impose order, justice and peace on earth, or would you rather he just revealed himself to your heart? Would you rather have him do for you what a king does or just be for you what a friend is? Would you prefer a God who grants all your requests or a God who simply shares all his thoughts with you?

What do you want more than anything else from your parish, your priests, the other members of the Church? Is it some particular service, or just that each one of us would be willing to sit down with you and share whatever we know and have experienced of Jesus Christ?

What are you willing to do for your parish? Contribute your hard-earned money generously to the works of the parish? Give of your limited time? Or will you give us first of all what is wanted more than anything else: will you share your experience of Jesus Christ? Will you reveal your heart?

Reflecting on This Week's Gospels

Thirty-Fourth Week of the Year

Pray daily: Lord Jesus, you came that we might "have life, and have it to the full." Let this desire of yours fill my heart. Fill me with desire to open myself to your life and to share it with others.

Monday: Luke 21:1-4. Jesus noticed a poor widow putting in two small coins. He said, "Truly I tell you, this poor widow has put in more than all of them." When does your offering at Mass best express the offering of your whole self?

Tuesday: Luke 21:5-11. "As for these things that you see, the days will come when not one stone will be left upon another; all will be thrown down." What do you do or experience in your religion that will last forever? What will not?

Wednesday: Luke 21:12-19. "By your endurance you will gain your souls." When are you most aware of "persevering"? When is it hardest to keep believing or living what you believe? What helps you the most then?

Thursday: Luke 21:20-28. "Now when these things begin to take place, stand up and raise your heads, because your redemption is drawing near." What in the life of Jesus or in the history of the Church tells you that when things are going badly you have the most reason to hope?

Friday: Luke 21:29-33. "When you see these things happening, know that the kingdom of God is near." What effect has opposition had on your religion? How does opposition make visible the faith, hope, love in our hearts?

Saturday: Luke 21:34-36. "Be alert at all times, praying that you may have the strength to escape all these things that will take place, and to stand before the Son of Man." When things are hard, does it help to look forward to the day when you will "stand before the Son of Man" in proven faith and fidelity?

Living This Week's Gospels

As Christian: Each day when you wake up, say to Jesus, "You are my friend." Then relate to him as friend.

As Disciple: Each time you have a decision to make, even a small one, ask Jesus' advice as you would ask a friend.

As Prophet: Display something visibly which shows that Jesus is your friend: a picture, cross, Scripture text, or whatever.

As Priest: Since you are the Body of Christ, show the friendship of Jesus to one person in some explicit way each day this week.

As King: Ask if any friends of Jesus whom you know are at odds with one another. Try to reconcile them.

SOLEMNITIES OF THE LORD

During the Season of the Year

Trinity Sunday (Sunday After Pentecost)

"In the Name of..."

Deuteronomy 4:32-34, 39-40; Romans 8:14-17;
Matthew 28:16-20

We baptize in the name of "Father, Son and Spirit." Many people are asking today whether the masculine images of God are too restrictive. Should we now begin to speak of God as "Father and Mother, Son and Daughter, and Spirit"?

The new *Catechism of the Catholic Church* reminds us that it is good to remember that the being of God is beyond human sexual distinctions. God is neither man nor woman, but God, and transcends human fatherhood and motherhood, even while being the origin and measure of both (#370).

In Scripture God is described sometimes, although rarely, in feminine terms. In Isaiah God says, "Can a woman forget her nursing child, / or show no compassion for the child of her womb? / Even these may forget, / yet I will not forget you"; and "As a mother comforts her child, so I will comfort you." And Jesus says of himself, "Jerusalem, Jerusalem, the city that kills the prophets and stones those who are sent to it! How often have I desired to gather your children together, as a hen gathers her brood under her wings, and you were not willing!"

For us who are alerted to the restrictiveness of thinking of God in any one gender, it can be helpful to reflect on the feminine characteristics of God. The psychologists tell us it is good for all of us to get in touch with that opposite side of our nature: our *animus* or *anima*. But by inspiring Saint Paul to describe the Church's relationship to Jesus as that of bride to bridegroom, God gave men a special reason for doing this. Theologically, every one of us who is baptized into the Church, the Bride of Christ, is a "bride in the Bride." Our gender usage gives women the advantage in relating to Jesus as spouse, because the correspondence of the language to their own sexuality makes it natural for them. On the levels of mystical union, if we judge from even male writers like Saint John of the Cross, for example, it is almost impossible not to put oneself in the bride's role with relationship to God. That would seem to put men at a disadvantage.

If we go beyond ("transcend") language, however, and look at God's self-revelation, even in and through the masculine human nature of Jesus, there are ways in which God takes on characteristics that are not only feminine, but more specifically, those of Bride, and to which even men can relate.

The way God chose to save the world through Jesus was not the way of authority and force which we often associate with maleness. It was through chosen powerlessness, vulnerability and surrender. Jesus came to "bear witness to the truth" in love. He came that we might "have life and have it to the full." He came to teach, to heal and to nourish, to nurture us: "The bread that I will give for the life of the world is my flesh." At the climax of his redemptive mission on earth he hung naked and vulnerable on the cross, his heart open for all time to all who would come to him.

In the Hebrew Scriptures God is present but hidden behind a "cloud" which "protects the glory of God against impure looks." Once a year the high priest could penetrate the temple veil which closed off access to the Holy of Holies. But now the temple veil is torn and Jesus has given us all access to deepest intimacy with God by "opening up a way through the veil of his own flesh." God invites us with passionate love to total knowledge and union.

God chose to be revealed as "Father" and "Son." We would be foolish to reject that imagery. But we need not restrict ourselves to it.

Note: You will need to check the Liturgical Calendar on page x to find out what week of the year follows Trinity Sunday this year. Once you know which week it is, you can find the weekday reflections after the article on that week's Sunday Gospel. For example, if the week following Trinity Sunday is the Eleventh Week of the Year, then locate the Eleventh Sunday of the Year and the weekday reflections for the Eleventh Week will follow.

Body and Blood of Christ (Corpus Christi)

Being the Body of Christ

Exodus 24:3-8; Hebrews 9:11-15; Mark 14:12-16, 22-26

After Pentecost we celebrate Trinity Sunday. This reminds us that the Holy Spirit came to form us into a community which is in the image of the Trinity. We all share in the one divine life of God, and we are called to become one in understanding, love and desire as the Father, Son and Spirit are one. We are a Church called to be a spiritual community, one whose primary focus is on achieving union of mind and will and heart with God and with each other.

Then we celebrate the feast of the Body and Blood of Christ: Corpus Christi. This reminds us that the Holy Spirit is sent to form us into a sacramental community, which means much more than just a community which gives and receives divine life through the seven sacraments.

Life given through a sacrament is always divine life given through a human action—a physical act of the Body of Christ on earth. God can give grace without using any human instrument, just by enlightening our minds with truth and moving our hearts by love. But when God gives grace through sacraments, it is always through the words and gestures of Christ's visible, human Body on earth. In the Church Jesus continues to speak with a human voice, to touch with human hands, to be present to us humanly, interacting in flesh and blood. To be a sacramental Church means to be the Body of Christ on earth and to accept what it means to be and to live as his Body.

The key to this and to all the sacraments is the Eucharist, the sacrament of Christ's Body and Blood. All the other sacraments either prepare us to receive the Eucharist and its graces—as Baptism, Reconciliation, and Confirmation do— or they strengthen us to live as Eucharist ourselves; that is, as the Body of Christ offered and given for the life of the world. Matrimony and Holy Orders empower us to "die to ourselves" in love by a committed sharing of all that we are, like bread that is broken, in the community of family or of Church. Anointing of the Sick empowers us to face the trials of sickness and death as Jesus himself did. The sacrament of the sick either overcomes sickness by healing it as Jesus did in his ministry or overcomes death by strengthening us to surrender to it in triumph as Jesus did on the cross.

The effect of Eucharist is to "change us into what we receive" (Saint Leo the Great). And what we become is the Body of Christ specifically offered in love and sacrifice for the life of the world. Four times before Communion Jesus is presented to us in the Eucharist as the "Lamb of God," the victim offered to take away the sins of the world. It is this Jesus which we deliver ourselves to become when we receive him in Communion. The Eucharist "is daily before our eyes as a representation of the passion of Christ. We hold it in our hands, we receive it in our mouths, we accept it in our hearts" (Saint Gaudentius).

To be a Eucharistic Church is to be a Church of priests offering themselves in Christ and with Christ as victims for the life of the world. This is something we do, not just when we physically die, but every day, every time we die to our own gratification, our own preferences, our own desires, to give ourselves in love and service to others. More deeply, we "die to ourselves" when we die to our fears, our compulsions, to all that holds us back from the total sharing of ourselves with others in love. As the Body of Christ, sharing in his mission on earth as sharers in his divine life, we share with other people our faith, our gifts of ministry, our material resources. We give expression to the faith, the hope, the love that are within us by grace. We let Jesus continue to express himself humanly in and through our human actions. This is what it is to be the Body of Christ and to be offered as Eucharist for the life of the world.

Note: You will need to check the Liturgical Calendar on page x to find out what week of the year follows the Feast of the Body and Blood of Christ this year. Once you know which week it is, you can find the weekday reflections after the article on that week's Sunday Gospel. For example, if the week following the Feast of the Body and Blood of Christ is the Twelfth Week of the Year, then locate the Twelfth Sunday of the Year and the weekday reflections for the Twelfth Week will follow.

Friday of Second Sunday After Pentecost
Sacred Heart of Jesus

Hosea 11:1, 3-4, 8-9; Ephesians 3:8-12,14-19; John 19:31-37

"[O]ne of the soldiers pierced his side with a spear, and at once blood and water came out." What does the open heart of Jesus on the cross say to you? What does he mean it to say?

OTHER SOLEMNITIES and FEASTS

Which Replace Sunday

February 2 • Presentation of the Lord

Presenting Jesus, Gifts, Us

Malachi 3:1-4; Hebrews 2:14-18; Luke 2:22-40

As Jesus was presented in the Temple, we present ourselves every time we celebrate Mass together. At the Presentation of the Gifts, when the bread and wine are brought up and placed on the altar, we are brought up. We are placing ourselves on the altar.

In some Protestant churches, especially during revivals, the preacher invites people to come forward after the preaching and accept Jesus as their Savior or give themselves to Jesus. It is a moment of choice in response to the word of God. And it is an adult choice: All who come up are declaring their faith personally and choosing as adults to live in relationship with Jesus Christ.

In the custom of the altar call the Protestants have kept, in a modified way, that moment of the Mass that we call the Offertory, which begins when the bread and wine are brought up and placed on the altar. Like the Catholic Offertory, the Protestant altar call takes place after the Scripture readings and preaching. And, like the Offertory, it expresses a personal, adult response. But there are some differences.

In the Catholic celebration, it is taken for granted that everyone who is participating in the eucharistic celebration has already been consecrated and made one with Jesus Christ by Baptism—and is, in fact, a priest, offering Jesus to the Father and offering himself or herself in Christ for the life of the world. Just to remind ourselves of this, we have restored an ancient custom: During one phase of the *Rite of Christian Initiation of Adults,* we ask all those who are preparing for Baptism to leave Mass before the Preparation of the Gifts. This is to make the point that in order really to participate in what takes place in the Liturgy of the Eucharist, one has to be—not just in intention but in fact—a "priest in the Priest," made one with Jesus by Baptism.

That is why we don't invite just a few people, those who have not yet done so, to come up and accept Jesus. The whole congregation has already accepted Jesus in Baptism. What we do is invite all present to reaffirm their Baptism, to recommit themselves by sending up the bread and the wine as symbols of themselves to be placed on the altar and changed into the Body and Blood of Christ. As we do this we express our participation in everything that will be expressed in the offering of the bread and wine during the rest of the eucharistic sacrifice. "Pray, brothers and sisters in Christ, that our sacrifice will be acceptable...." And the people answer, "May the Lord accept the sacrifice at your hands"—the sacrifice we make of ourselves in union with Jesus Christ. We offer ourselves with him and in him, as his real Body on earth.

The offering we make of ourselves by placing ourselves on the altar under the form of bread and wine has a very precise meaning. It is not just an act of accepting Jesus in general as our Savior, or of giving ourselves to Jesus in some vague way. In the Offertory we join ourselves to Jesus precisely and explicitly to be offered with him as Lamb of God. By identifying ourselves with Jesus offered in the Mass, we identify ourselves with everything he did and expressed on the cross.

We die to ourselves and to sin to live in Christ. We go down into the grave with Christ as we went down into the waters of Baptism and we rise with him, leaving all our sins behind, to live a new life on earth. In Paul's words (see Romans 12:1-2), we offer our bodies as a living sacrifice to God. This means that wherever our bodies are, we are sacrificed, offered, committed to doing whatever Christ wants to do through us. We live now, no longer for ourselves, but that Christ may live through us. We live for his mission.

June 24 • Birth of John the Baptist

Luke 1:57-66, 80

"Fear came over all their neighbors, and all these things were talked about throughout the entire hill country of Judea." How, as a community, do we nurture in each other awe at God's working in each person and in the Church?

June 29 • Peter and Paul, Apostles

Matthew 16:13-19

He said to them, "But who do you say that I am?" What do your actions say Jesus is for you?

August 6 • Transfiguration of the Lord

Mark 9:2-10

"Then a cloud overshadowed them, and from the cloud there came a voice, 'This is my Son, the Beloved; listen to him!'" What did the disciples appreciate more in Jesus after the transfiguration? Do you "listen" to him in a way that shows the same appreciation?

August 15 • Assumption of the Blessed Virgin

The Triumph of Human Vulnerability

Revelation 11:19a, 12:1-6a, 10ab; 1 Corinthians 15:20-27;
Luke 1:39-56

All three readings for the Feast of the Assumption celebrate God's victory over sin and death, over all that is evil and life-diminishing for the human race. And all three emphasize the role that human nature, in all its weakness, plays in this victory.

A woman "crying out in the pangs of childbirth" is the image of total helplessness and awesome power. On the one hand, nothing can stop the birthing process; she must surrender to it, cooperate with it or die. On the other hand, through the weakness of her flesh, through the surrender of her body to the inevitable, she is going to accomplish the greatest thing any human person can do: She is going to bring a human being to life. This is an exercise of power unsurpassed in human existence.

This is the image God chose to express the reality of the Church on earth. On the one hand, we are as helpless and vulnerable as a woman in labor, undergoing pain, suffering from the resistance of our own flesh and from the opposition of the world around us as we labor to "bring Christ to full stature" (see Ephesians 4:13). On the other hand, we are actually bringing about God's presence in human flesh on earth and establishing the reign of God in human affairs.

The Assumption—the taking up of Mary's body into heaven that exempted her from the disintegration of the grave—is a sign and preview of the triumph of fragile human flesh over all that threatens our existence on earth. It is God's assurance to us that these bodies of ours, so vulnerable to sickness, injury and death, will share in the resurrection of Jesus. Jesus rose as the "first fruits" of a human race delivered from the power of sin and death. His resurrection is a sign that God has given to him all "sovereignty, authority and power," that the reign of God will be realized. Mary's assumption is a sign that the human race will share—in body as well as in soul—in his victory and his heavenly glory, just as we have shared in the weakness and humiliation he accepted on earth.

The human race came under the power of sin and death when a man and a woman, Adam and Eve, freely chose to sin. Jesus broke this power by freely choosing as God to become a member of this sinful race and by freely surrendering himself to death. But he chose to become human only through the free surrender of a woman who agreed to give him flesh—and who, standing under the cross, accepted with him to endure the birth pangs again as her heart was torn open with his flesh and the human race reborn. Mary had to be under the cross. And she had to be there, not just as a spectator, but actively offering her Son to the Father for the life of the world. She had to join him in his act of priesthood and offer him as he offered himself, just as all of us do at Mass. She had to take part.

The Assumption, by proclaiming the share human beings have in the Resurrection of Jesus, also proclaims the share human beings have in the redeeming work, the sacrifice of Jesus. Like Mary, all of us who have "offered our bodies as a living sacrifice to God" in Baptism have agreed to give flesh to Jesus on earth. We have consented to become his Body so that he may continue in us his human presence in the world, and through our actions continue his ministry. Like Mary, we are called to embrace his way of redeeming the world through vulnerability, through human powerlessness, through sacrifice and the offering of ourselves for others in love—especially for those who violate our rights, oppress us and kill us. Like Mary, we have agreed to give our bodies, our "flesh for the life of the world," so that in us Jesus may continue to live and act, to give himself up to death in love, to redeem the world.

Mary triumphed through surrender. In celebrating her Assumption we celebrate the triumph of fragile humanity, of vulnerable human flesh, over all the death-dealing power of this world and over all those who claim the authority to direct the course of human affairs in disassociation from God. With Mary we celebrate freedom from all fear of death. We proclaim the greatness of the Lord, for he who is mighty has done great things, even through the lowliness of his servant. Holy is his name!

September 14 • Exaltation of the Cross

John 3:13-17

"Indeed, God did not send the Son into the world to condemn the world, but in order that the world might be saved through him." How can you respond to people who annoy you in a way that saves and does not condemn?

We Are All Saints

Revelation 7:2-4, 9-14; 1 John 3:1-3; Matthew 5:1-12a

T he word *saint* comes from the Latin word for "holy"
(*sanctus*), but it doesn't mean what we may take it
to mean. We think that a "holy" person is a virtuous
person, someone who seldom if ever sins. But the real
meaning of *holy* is "consecrated, set aside, separated from
the ordinary."

God is the "holy of holies," the absolutely Holy One,
because God is by nature separate, apart, different from
everyone and everything—while at the same time close to
and most intimately involved with everyone and everything.
God is in a category all his own—or more accurately, God
is not in any category; God just is. There is God and, on a
completely different level, there is everything else.

The Jews were holy because God chose them and set
them apart to be his special people: "For I am the LORD who
brought you up from the land of Egypt, to be your God; you
shall be holy, for I am holy" (Leviticus 11:45). The sabbath
observance was a reminder of this: "You shall keep my
sabbaths, for this is a sign between me and you throughout
your generations, given in order that you may know that I,
the LORD, sanctify you" (Exodus 31:13).

Because the Church is the continuation of the chosen
people, Saint Peter calls us "a chosen race, a royal
priesthood, a holy nation" (see 1 Peter 2:9). We are holy
as a Church, however, not only because God has set us apart
for special relationship, but also because this relationship is
a sharing in God's own divine life by grace. God has joined
us to the divine self by making us members of the Body of
Christ, "the high priest, holy, blameless, undefiled, separated
from sinners, and exalted above the heavens" (see Hebrews
7:26). By Baptism we have "become Christ." And so we are

holy—different, set apart, consecrated—as he is holy.

Jesus came down to earth to be one of us, like us in every way except sin. Jesus,

> though he was in the form of God,
>> did not regard equality with God
>> as something to be exploited,
> but emptied himself,
>> taking the form of a slave,
>> being born in human likeness.
> And being found in human form,
>> he humbled himself,
>> and became obedient to the point of death—
>> even death on a cross.
> Therefore, God also highly exalted him
>> and gave him the name
>> that is above every name,
> so that at the name of Jesus
>> every knee should bend,
>> in heaven and on earth and under the earth,
> and every tongue should confess
>> that Jesus Christ is Lord
>> to the glory of God the Father (Philippians 2:6-11).

We proclaim in the *Gloria* of the Mass, "For you alone are the Holy One, you alone are the Lord, you alone are the Most High, Jesus Christ...." But now God has made us holy in Christ. By Baptism we were "separated" from this world; we died to it in Christ and we came back into it as his risen Body to continue what he came to do—or, better, to let him continue it in us. Saint Peter constantly calls the members of the Church "the holy ones" and urges, "as he who called you is holy, be holy yourselves in all your conduct; for it is written, 'You shall be holy, for I am holy'"(1 Peter 1:15).

That is what we are. We have been set apart and consecrated through union with Jesus Christ to do his work in the world. That is why we must live his life in the world; live it as he lived it. Those whom we celebrate as "saints" are simply those who have shown us in every age—in every walk of life, and under every set of circumstances—how to do this.

In the Beatitudes Jesus gives us a thumbnail sketch of the mindset we need to live as Christ. The only way to understand the Beatitudes is to see them as the attitudes and values of those who are holy—set apart and consecrated to be different from what is considered normal on earth. For people who take life on earth at face value, it is definitely not a blessing to be poor, sorrowing or persecuted. The meek don't inherit the earth; they lose it to the strong and ruthless. And those who go to work every day hungering and thirsting above all for uprightness, seeking purely the kingdom of God, will probably not have their pockets filled at the end of the day.

But they are being filled—with all the fullness of God. They are receiving what they have been set apart to receive, because they are giving what they have been set apart to give. And it is one and the same thing: the life of God, life in abundance, life to the full. That is what Jesus came into this world to give.

November 2 • Commemoration of the Faithful Departed (All Souls)

John 6:37-40

"This is indeed the will of my Father, that all who see the Son and believe in him may have eternal life; and I will raise them up on the last day." Does God desire your salvation more than you do? Does Jesus? How do you know this?

November 9 • Dedication of the Lateran Basilica

John 2:13-22

"Making a whip of cords [Jesus] drove all of them out of the Temple, both the sheep and the cattle... [He said] 'Take these things out of here! Stop making my father's house a marketplace!'" How much respect do you have for church buildings as such? Why? How do you personally show respect when you are in church?

FEASTS and SAINTS' DAYS

January 25 • Conversion of Paul, Apostle

Mark 16:15-18

Jesus said, "Go into all the world and proclaim the good news to the whole creation." Why do these words call you into relationship with every other person on earth? How do you make that relationship real?

February 22 • Chair of Peter, Apostle

Matthew 16:13-19

When Jesus went into the region of Caesarea Philippi, he asked his disciples, "Who do people say that the Son of Man is? ...Who do you say that I am?" How would you answer that question? What is Jesus for you? God? Friend? Teacher? Leader? Spouse? How do you usually relate to Jesus?

March 19 • Joseph, Husband of Mary

Matthew 1:16, 18-21, 24a

"Now the birth of Jesus the Messiah took place in this way. When his mother Mary had been engaged to Joseph, but before they lived together, she was found to be with child from the Holy Spirit." Joseph agreed to have no sexual relations with Mary, his true wife, for as long as he lived. It was his contribution to saving the world. Do you think it was worth it? How are the sacrifices in your life the price you pay for helping to save the world? Is it worth what it costs you?

March 25 • The Annunciation of the Lord

Luke 1:26-38

"And now, you will conceive in your womb and bear a son, and you will name him Jesus." Do you believe you are called as truly as Mary was to conceive thoughts in your head through the seed of Christ's word, and bear fruit by giving them flesh in action? How do you open yourself to his words?

April 25 • Mark, Evangelist

Mark 16:15-20

"And they went out and proclaimed the good news everywhere, while the Lord worked with them and confirmed the message by the signs that accompanied it." Is this a description of your life? How are you exercising priesthood?

May 3 • Philip and James, Apostles

John 14:6-14

"Very truly I tell you, the one who believes in me will also do the works that I do and, in fact, will do greater works than these, because I am going to the Father." What are the "works of Jesus" that you do as his priest?

May 14 • Matthias, Apostle

John 15:9-17

"I have called you friends, because I made known to you everything I have heard from my Father." How do you recognize someone's friends? Is it obvious you are Christ's friend?

May 31 • Visitation

Luke 1:39-56

Elizabeth said to Mary, "And blessed is she who believed that there would be a fulfillment of what was spoken to her by the Lord." What divine promises to you do you find hard to believe? See Matthew 21:22 and John 15:16.

June 11 • Barnabas, Apostle

Matthew 10:7-13

"As you go, proclaim the good news, 'The kingdom of heaven has come near.' Cure the sick, raise the dead, cleanse the lepers, cast out demons." Which of these actions is an example of acting as prophet? As priest? As king?

July 3 • Thomas, Apostle

John 20:24-29

Then Jesus said to Thomas, "Put your finger here and see my hands. Reach out your hand and put it in my side. Do not doubt but believe." In how many ways has Jesus met you more than halfway when you had little faith?

July 22 • Mary Magdalene

John 20:1-2, 11-18

"Jesus said to her, 'Mary!' She turned and said to him in Hebrew, 'Rabbouni,' (which means Teacher)." What name does Jesus use when he talks to you? What name do you use when you talk to him? Why?

July 29 • Martha

Luke 10:38-42

"Martha, Martha, you are worried and distracted by many things; there is need of only one thing. Mary has chosen the better part, which will not be taken away from her." What worries distract you from God? How could these unite you to God?

August 10 • Lawrence, Deacon and Martyr

John 12:24-26

Jesus said, "Those who love their life lose it, and those who hate their life in this world will keep it for eternal life." What are you willing to do to other people in order to preserve your life? Your livelihood? Your standard of living?

August 24 • Bartholomew, Apostle

John 1:45-51

"Nathanael said to [Philip], 'Can anything good come out of Nazareth?' Philip said to him, 'Come and see.'" What external signs did Jesus use to show people he was important? What did he not use?

September 8 • Birth of Mary

Matthew 1:1-16, 18-23

"When his mother Mary had been engaged to Joseph, but before they lived together, she was found to be with child...." How many people in Nazareth judged Mary for being pregnant before marriage without asking her any questions? What would they have learned if they had?

September 15 • Our Lady of Sorrows

Luke 2:33-35

"Then Simeon blessed them and said to his mother Mary, 'This child is destined for the falling and the rising of many in Israel, and to be a sign that will be opposed....'" How much opposition would you experience if, every time you heard anyone criticized, you spoke aobut the Christian call to forgive and to love?

September 21 • Matthew, Apostle and Evangelist

Matthew 9:9-13

"As Jesus was walking along, he saw a man called Matthew sitting at the tax booth; and he said to him, 'Follow me.' And he got up and followed him." In everything you do, are you most aware of yourself as being a disciple and follower of Jesus?

September 29 • Michael, Gabriel and Raphael, Archangels

John 1:47-51

"Nathanael replied, 'Rabbi, you are the Son of God. You are the King of Israel!'" Do you really believe that everything Jesus teaches is a way to greater happiness and fulfillment, even on this earth? What follows from this?

October 2 • Guardian Angels

Matthew 18:1-5, 10

Jesus said, "Whoever becomes humble like this child is the greatest in the kingdom of heaven." Do you believe you will be happier by becoming humble (having no more prestige than a little child) or by becoming important? Why?

October 18 • Luke, Evangelist

Luke 10:1-9

Jesus said, "Whatever house you enter, first say, 'Peace to this house!'" In your dealings with other people is peace with mutual understanding and affection your first priority? What do you focus on first?

October 28 • Simon and Jude, Apostles

Luke 6:12-16

"And when day came, [Jesus] called his disciples and chose twelve of them, whom he also named apostles." *Disciple* means "learner." *Apostle* means "one who is sent." Which are you? What visible actions in your life show you are each of these?

November 30 • Andrew, Apostle

Matthew 4:18-22

"Immediately they left the boat and their father, and followed him." How is following Jesus different from just keeping God's law? What are you willing to leave to follow him more closely?

December 12 • Our Lady of Guadalupe

Luke 1:38-47

Elizabeth cried out, "Blessed are you among women, and blessed is the fruit of your womb." How are you blessed? How does your life bear divine fruit?